Woodworking for Young Children

Patsy Skeen
University of Georgia

Anita Payne Garner
Gainesville (Georgia) Junior College

Sally Cartwright
Community Nursery School
Tenants Harbor, Maine

National Association for the Education of Young Children
Washington, D.C.

Photo credits
Jean Berlfein 28, 43
Philip Biscuiti, Connecticut College 58
Faith Bowlus 48
Sally Cartwright x, 4, 21, 24, 36, 49, 50, 56, 57
Special thanks to Alice Davis and City and Country
School who made possible the photograph on page x
illustrating child-initiated woodworking activities
integrated with social studies and block play.
Lila Lasky 38
Clyde Mueller cover, 60
Barbara Rios 54
Frank D. Torre 30
Photograph from *Woodworking for Kids* by
Frank D. Torre. Copyright © 1978 by Frank D. Torre.
Reprinted by permission of Doubleday & Company, Inc.

The National Association for the Education of Young
Children attempts through its publications program to
provide a forum for discussion of major issues and ideas
in our field. We hope to provoke thoughts and promote
professional growth. The views expressed or implied are
not necessarily those of the Association.

Library of Congress Catalog Card Number: 84-61512
ISBN Catalog Number: 0-912674-85-7
NAEYC #122

Printed in the United States of America

To Fan Brooke and D. Keith Osborn for their years of commitment to young children and for their support and confidence in us.

P. S. and A. P. G.

To my dad, Henry Willcox, who taught his sons and daughters to be caring, lifelong woodworkers.

S. C.

Contents

A C K N O W L E D G M E N T S

I would like to thank Norman Tate, designer and
woodworker, Port Clyde, Maine, and also
Ed Glaser of Tenants Harbor, Maine, shipwright.

Sally Cartwright
Tenants Harbor, Maine

Introduction

"When I learned that I had been hired at the day care center, I was very excited. The school felt good. The children and teachers were busy and seemed to really like each other. This was just the place for me. But my fourth day at work was traumatic—I was asked to supervise the new woodworking center. I didn't know a thing about woodworking. My only experience with wood and tools had been smashing my fingers and looking for dropped nails while putting up pictures. How on earth would I get through a woodworking experience with children?"

Feelings of fear and ineptness, as well as lack of experience and understanding of tools and woodworking, are common for many adults in our culture. Woodworking *can* be frustrating and dangerous for inexperienced adults. However woodworking does not require great strength, and teachers who take the time to learn about it can provide satisfying learning experiences for young children. The first purpose of this book is to provide information about tools and woodworking for adults who work with young children so that they can become comfortable offering woodworking activities. The second purpose is to provide teaching suggestions for woodworking with young children. Chapter 1 discusses the value of woodworking for children. Chapter 2 covers the selection, use, and care of materials and equipment. Chapter 3 includes ideas for setting up the woodworking center. Chapter 4 emphasizes the teacher's attitude and role in planning, including matching activities to children's developmental abilities, supporting the child, ensuring safety, and setting specific limits. Chapter 5 suggests ways to resolve difficulties and ways to integrate woodworking activities with the development of the whole child. An annotated bibliography on woodworking for children and adults completes the book.

If you are an experienced woodworker, you may want to conduct workshops for teachers and parents to help them develop their skills and an understanding of the values of woodworking. Suggestions for conducting a woodworking workshop for teachers and parents are offered beginning on page 77.

Woodworking builds children's sense of competence through boldly three-dimensional creative action and mastery.

CHAPTER 1
Why Offer Woodworking?

Woodworking is a splendid activity for young children to learn more about themselves and the world around them if the teacher enhances children's initiative, knows how children develop and learn, and truly *sees* each individual child. Through woodworking, children can broaden and refine their cognitive, physical, emotional, and social skills. Table 1 contains a useful list of goals for children's learning through woodworking. For convenience these are grouped under these four familiar categories. However, the interrelationship of these aspects of child development is as important as the aspects themselves (Biber et al. 1977). Children learn best through their own pursuit of experience (Dewey 1938; Piaget 1964), and children who work well with tools and wood confirm the many interrelated values of this type of purposeful learning.

Good woodworking teachers bring a "fine blend of strength and delicacy to [the] job" and "need to be ... so secure ... that [they] can function with principles rather than with prescriptions, ... can exert authority without requiring submission, ... can work experimentally but not at random, [and] ... can admit mistakes without feeling humiliated" (Snyder and Biber 1965, pp. 6–7).

These adult qualities are especially needed when uniting children with tools and wood because the potential for emotional and physical hurt is always present (see Chapter 4). When a child's painstaking construction splits in two, the frustration and/or defeat may be devastating, while misuse of a hammer may be extremely dangerous. There is much indeed to know about children, teaching, tools, and wood. However, when you offer woodworking in an appropriately planned and caring environment, the results may be rewarding beyond measure.

Woodworking builds self-esteem through competence

A child—or an adult—who masters the skill of driving a nail is gaining a sense of positive self-esteem. And later, perhaps while constructing a working

Table 1.
Goals for children's learning through woodworking.

Cognitive
1. To develop relationship thinking: cause and effect; relatedness of things, feelings, activities; single attribute and cross-set classification.
2. To understand number concepts through concrete use of counting, one-to-one correspondence, awareness of simple shapes, comparison of size, experience with metric measure in three dimensions.
3. To know and use wood and tools with purpose and satisfaction.
4. To experience joy in discovery, in active learning, in striving to find out information children need for their own purposes.
5. To increase communication skills through talking about woodworking and tools, reading directions or labels, writing reports about woodworking, drawing scaled plans.
6. To solve problems through divergent thinking and planning creatively with three-dimensional wood constructs.

Physical
1. To develop and coordinate large and small muscles, delight in movement and rhythm, feel competent in motor control and skill achievement.
2. To master physical woodworking skills: measuring, hammering, sawing, planing, filing, finishing.
3. To expand senses through smells, textures, and sounds of woodworking.

Emotional
1. To build strong, positive feelings about self.
2. To foster ability to meet new situations well.

continued on next page

drawbridge for group block play, a child builds upon that same self-esteem (see photo on p. x). An individual's positive self-image is basic to successful living; a sense of competence—ego strength—is essential to the child's best learning, and it is essential to the process of creativity (Biber et al. 1977). Woodworking, when children and the process are handled with care, builds children's sense of competence through boldly three-dimensional creative action and mastery.

Table 1, continued

3. To learn to sustain interest and overcome frustration successfully.
4. To become open and sensitive to feelings in self and others such as humor, sadness, tension, anger, excitement, and peacefulness.
5. To expand intuitive learning through self-directed creativity such as feeling and testing hunches about performance of wood, tools, co-workers.
6. To enhance personality integration through satisfying firsthand experience with wood and tools.

Social
1. To cooperate with others which leads to viable democratic process.
2. To learn to grasp and follow rules for the safety of others as well as for oneself.
3. To accept differences among children with understanding and compassion.
4. To achieve satisfying friendships.
5. To sense responsibility to the group and status gained from this.
6. To experience joy in cooperative responsibility and group accomplishment.
7. To achieve a deeply felt awareness that authority and group structure can promote individual fulfillment.

These goals are guidelines along which children may venture in their own way and at their own pace.

When a young carpenter builds a bridge for group block play, the building *process* is more important than the final product, just as the process is with most of the work of learning for young children. Notice in the photo on p. x how incomplete the woodworking is. Only the opening span and abutments are carpentry. The rest of the bridge is made of blocks. Yet the carpentry as a contribution to an ongoing creative process, the group's work of learning, is significant in two ways: (1) it directly enhances everyone's learning (not least the teacher's) of road and river traffic and cooperative endeavor—cognitive and social acquisitions, and (2) it augments the bridge builder's feelings of self-worth through the experience of contributing to the group's need and fulfilling that need. No verbal praise could or should mean as much.

Woodworking enhances physical, cognitive, and social skills

Self-esteem grows from competence in many skills and many roles: using large and small muscles to hammer, saw, or screw a hinge in place; describing the width, height, or shape of a project; learning about cause and effect; joining

In woodworking as in block play, using *information they have found through exploration and firsthand experience, children can build a life-long style of effective learning.*

two pieces of wood in one-to-one correspondence; appreciating the smell and texture of various woods; working hard with others—even designing a bridge so the children's cars and trucks can cross the waterway and child-made boats can pass through. However, this child's bridge crosses more than a pretend river. It is a social bridge as well, for it enables the child to interact on important levels with classmates: getting along through argument and trial, holding forth, hearing others, giving way, and finally solving a serious problem in their play.

This kind of problem-solving process, intimately related to woodworking, reflects the real world young children discover beyond school. Thus, in woodworking as in block play, *using* information they have found through exploration and firsthand experience, children can build a lifelong style of effective learning (Cartwright 1971).

The bridge example tells much about the rewards of woodworking. Not only does a child gain self-esteem, enhance cognitive and physical skills, and build emotional and social strength through accomplishment and from meeting a group need, but woodworking often supports social studies and geography, each a part of *good block play* for ages three to seven (Cartwright 1974, 1976; Hirsch 1984).

Many times woodworking enhances other areas of the young child's learning. With a bit of cedar shingle, a four-year-old makes a wind-directed weather vane. A five-year-old, broadly copying a compass, makes *north, south, east,* and *west* on wood struts below the revolving vane. Learning about the science of weather is thus enhanced by wood. Such deep involvement, such creative and purposeful action on the part of children gives them incentive to explore weather, wind, and mechanics.

Woodworking encourages creativity

Creativity is most likely to be enhanced when the teacher provides materials, technical assistance when needed, and sets limits—especially those involving safety—but allows children to experiment as they wish. As technical skills increase, children can use more advanced tools, increasing possibilities for creativity and self-directed learning.

When children use precut kits such as those for birdhouses or when teachers provide models to be copied, children are not being creative. Preschool children do not have the skills to build these kinds of projects and become frustrated when forced to try. The likely results of such frustration—tears, anger, quitting, and feelings of unworthiness—are not productive for teachers or children. For details about the creative process and how it can be fostered, see Lasky and Mukerji (1980).

*   *   *   *   *

Woodworking is a source for both learning and enjoyment. Traditional curriculum areas—reading, language arts, writing, math, science, music, art, social studies—can be an integral part of the learning-by-doing experiences of woodworking. The needs of the whole child—cognitive, physical, emotional, and social—can be met as well. If children's woodworking experiences are to be rewarding for adults and children however, it is important to choose the correct equipment and know how to orchestrate learning activities.

CHAPTER 2

Materials and Equipment: Selection, Use, and Care

Woodworking with children involves materials, tools, and children. The quality of the wood and equipment combined with the children's approach and skill determine the process and product of woodworking. This chapter introduces wood and its qualities, typical processed wood byproducts, tools and accessories, and metric measurement.

Wood

How does the growing process of trees affect the woodworker? Logs are cut from the stem or trunk of a tree. The cross section of a tree trunk (see Figure 1) illustrates how a tree grows. The inner part of the tree, called the **heartwood,** is the strong, darker, stable part of the tree which is no longer growing. In contrast, the **sapwood,** or the part of the trunk surrounding the heartwood, is the growing part of the tree. The sapwood carries water and dissolved mineral salts, called the **sap,** from the roots through the trunk to the leaves. The sapwood is softer and more likely to warp and be harmed by insects and fungi than the heartwood (Lawrence 1979).

On a smoothly sawn end of every log cut from a tree trunk, you will see **annual growth rings.** Each ring marks a single year's growing season. Each growing season a new layer of wood, called the **cambium,** grows on the outside of the sapwood layer, just inside the bark of the tree. More sap rises through the sapwood during the spring than during the summer. The new wood cells formed in the spring are larger and lighter in color than those formed in summer. This difference in size and color between the spring and summer wood cells causes the alternate light and dark rings which are called the annual growth rings. By counting the rings to see how old a tree is, children can begin to develop an understanding of life cycles and a respect for the need to conserve and replenish natural resources. An accurate measure of the tree's full age must be done near the ground to get the earliest years of

Figure 1. Cross section of tree trunk

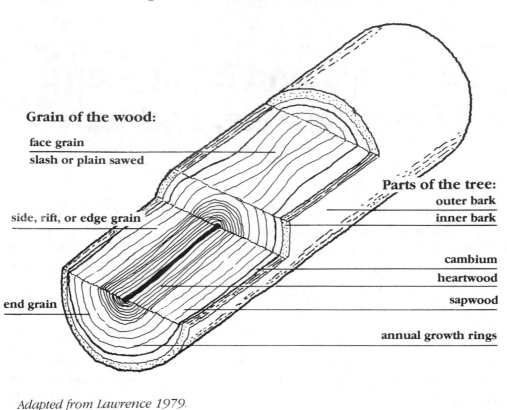

Grain of the wood:

face grain

slash or plain sawed

side, rift, or edge grain

end grain

Parts of the tree:

outer bark

inner bark

cambium

heartwood

sapwood

annual growth rings

Adapted from Lawrence 1979.

growth. The teacher and/or children may be able to locate a tree stump nearby so that children can observe firsthand how these rings occur in nature.

Wood grain is the lengthwise pattern in the wood caused by the tree's annual growth rings. Grain displays three distinct patterns (see Figure 1). **End grain** is the cross-sectional pattern of growth rings at either end of a log or board. **Side, rift,** or **edge grain** shows the lengthwise pattern of wood fibers side by side, fairly straight, and parallel. **Face grain** also runs lengthwise but shows a pattern of broad curves made by the growth rings as they go in and out of the flat plane made when the log was sawed (Adkins 1973). Grain is the lengthwise fiber of the wood which gives strength to boards. Wood splits along the fiber or with the grain and may weaken any wood construction if not considered carefully. Children can drive several nails into a board with pronounced grain to see how wood splits.

Kinds of trees

There are two types of trees in the United States temperate zone. The **evergreens** or cone-bearing (coniferous) needle-leaf trees do not shed their leaves and are known as **softwoods.** One exception is the larch, also called tamarack or hackmatack, which is an evergreen that sheds its leaves. In contrast, **broadleaf** or deciduous trees shed their leaves each fall and are known as **hardwoods.** *Softwoods* and *hardwoods* refer only to these two kinds of trees, not necessarily to softness or hardness of the wood. For example, some hardwoods such as poplar are softer than softwoods such as southern yellow pine. Table 2 lists the major evergreen and deciduous trees, as well as sheet board products which are likely to be available in the United States, along with their characteristics and suitability for young children's woodworking.

White pine, poplar, cedar, and spruce are best, in that order, for young children to use. Teak and mahoganies are also easy to work and most attractive when oiled or varnished, but they are imported and can be very expensive.

Teachers and parents often are limited to using free scrap wood. Preschoolers are not product-oriented and may use a great deal of wood to practice sawing and nailing. For this reason, testing clean wood scraps to determine the merits of each wood is recommended. After sawing and nailing sample pieces, teachers can decide what to use with children.

For skilled workers older than nine years, walnut and oak deserve special mention. Black walnut is a beautiful, semi-hard, relatively nonsplitting wood, especially fine for carving. Oak, although hard, is widely available and very strong.

Children can learn a great deal about different types of trees by studying those in the neighborhood or in a nearby park. Help children identify the variety in shapes of needles or leaves, branching patterns, and seasonal changes. Fallen leaves, acorns, sweet gum balls, or twigs may be gathered by the children for bouquets or collages. Teachers can extend the study of growth to people and other plants, comparing changes and growth rates. The possibilities for studying about trees and ecology are vast and can be incorporated into nearly every aspect of children's learning.

Wood qualities

Wood that has been cut into boards is called lumber and is graded according to quality. The major reasons for differences in quality are listed here. Because conditions and/or defects vary, every piece of wood is unique even if it is from the same kind of tree.

Table 2.
Wood and wood products grown and manufactured in the
United States.

Type	Characteristics	Suitability for young children
Evergreens		
Cedar	Used for shingles, posts, chests, and boats. Resists decay and insects. Western varieties are lightweight, weak, and soft with a coarse texture. Eastern varieties are stronger, with a uniform texture.	Recommended when white pine is not available.
Douglas fir	Commonly used for structural girders, pilings, plywood, furniture, and pulpwood. Strong, fairly hard, heavy, and stiff. More difficult to work with than white pine.	Not recommended, except with children age eight and older for large structural work such as sawhorses, tree houses, and sheds. Two- and three-year-olds can use scrap fir, however, as a firm base for constructions with glue and for nailing and sawing practice.
Hemlock	Light in weight, moderately hard, and weak. Tends to split, does not hold nails or take paint well.	Not recommended except scraps for sawing practice.
White pine (eastern, western, sugar)	Used for carpentry and building. Easily worked, lightweight, moderately strong, and soft. Holds nails, glue, and paint well. More expensive than other pines.	Highly recommended.
Southern yellow pine (longleaf, slash, short leaf, and loblolly)	Used in heavy structures and framing because of its availability and strength. Generally harder than other pines and heavy. Has a tendency to split during nailing and does not hold paint well. Source of turpentine and resins.	Not recommended.

continued on next page

Table 2, continued

Type	Characteristics	Suitability for young children
Redwood	Used for outdoor furniture, shingles, siding, etc. Expensive. Lightweight, fairly strong, easy to work, resistant to decay, holds paint well. Splits easily.	Acceptable.
Spruce (white, black, red, Sitka, and Engelmann)	Used for framing. Easy to work, light, soft, average strength. Takes nails well.	Desirable.

Broadleaf

Type	Characteristics	Suitability for young children
Oaks, birches, hickory, ash	Suitable for flooring, paneling, doors, professional cabinet work, marine uses. Heavy, hard, strong, and of reasonable cost. Difficult to work; guide holes must be used for nailing and drilling.	Not recommended, except for experienced workers when strength, special finish, and/or marine use are required.
Maple, cherry	Used for furniture and woodenware. Heavy, hard, strong, and stiff woods—not easy to work. Difficult to nail and saw. Expensive.	Not recommended for young children, but experienced woodworkers may want to try such woods.
Poplar	Fairly strong, slightly softer than white pine, easy to work. Takes and holds nails well.	Desirable.
Black walnut	Tougher than white pine, but beautiful, nonsplitting, and especially good for carving. Expensive.	Recommended for skilled, older students.

continued on next page

Table 2, continued

Type	Characteristics	Suitability for young children
Sheet board products		
Insulation board (also called fiberboard or soft wallboard)	Used for insulating ceilings or walls or as bulletin boards. Light, soft, flexible, and weak. Flexibility binds the sawblade when sawing. Easy to glue and nail. Does not hold nails well and breaks easily.	Recommended for beginners and bulletin boards.
Hardboard (Masonite)	Used for shelf backing, cheap walls. Has good lateral strength and is harder and heavier than insulation board. Moderately easy to saw and nail to wood frames. Glues well.	Not recommended except for shelf backing and as a base for three-dimensional maps (such as papier mâché or Plasticine).
Chipboard (also called particleboard or flakeboard)	Formed by bonding wood particles into sheets. Used for underlaving floors and for shelving. Easily sawed and glues well, but tends to split or break when nailed on the edges.	Recommended for some child constructions.

continued on next page

Sawing boards from logs. Plain sawn and tangentially sawn boards (see Figure 2) are usually slightly cheaper, often have lovely wide grain, and can be cut to greater widths. But these boards are more likely to warp, shrink, and splinter from the face than quarter sawn wood. Quarter sawn wood often has a more reliable surface and is less likely to warp and twist. It is also often stronger if the grain is close and straight, and it generally holds paint better than plain sawn wide-grain lumber.

Table 2, continued

Type	Characteristics	Suitability for young children
Plywood	Used for subflooring, siding, paneling, and shelving. Heavy, moderately hard, and much stronger than other board products. Difficult to nail into edge without splitting but nails through face to other wood easily.	Recommended primarily for use by older children.
Doweling	Hard, splits easily, difficult to nail, but can be glued into a hole drilled to its exact size.	Useful for boat stacks and masts glued into correct-size holes. Diameters of 12.5mm (1/2″) and 25mm (1″) are best.

Information clarified and adapted by Sally Cartwright.

Seasoning. When a living tree is cut down or **felled,** it is called **green** wood. Green wood contains a great deal of moisture, especially the life-giving sap in the sapwood. Before wood is cut and fitted for use, this moisture should be either dried out in a heated kiln or air-dried indoors or out—a process called **seasoning.** If wood is not seasoned, it will dry after it has been cut and fitted for use, causing problems of shrinkage, pulling away at the joints, warping (curving), and checking (splitting). If drying is uneven, the knots will

Figure 2. Sawing methods

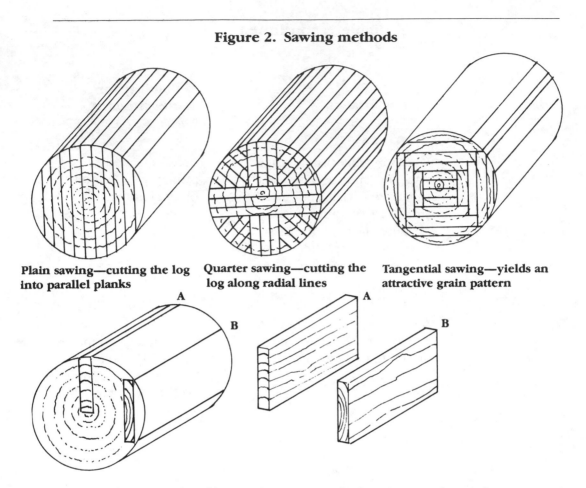

Plain sawing—cutting the log into parallel planks

Quarter sawing—cutting the log along radial lines

Tangential sawing—yields an attractive grain pattern

The grain pattern produced by various sawing methods varies according to the position of the piece within the log.
From Lawrence 1979.

become loose. For all of these reasons, seasoned wood is far better for most purposes than green wood. Seasoned lumber is also lighter and easier to work than green lumber. Because it can be precisely controlled, kiln dried lumber is better than air dried. The moisture content (MC) is a measure of the amount of water (sap and moisture from surrounding air) in the wood. Kiln dried lumber often has less than 10 percent MC and is best for children if available.

Rough sawn and dressed lumber. The circular saws with large teeth which cut logs into lumber cause rough and splintery surfaces on the boards.

Figure 3. Common wood defects

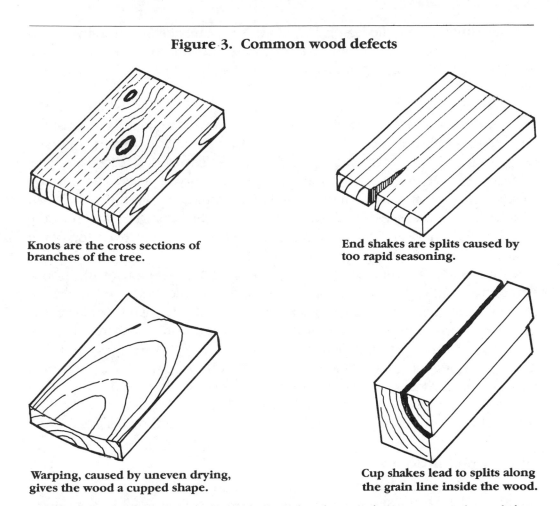

Knots are the cross sections of branches of the tree.

End shakes are splits caused by too rapid seasoning.

Warping, caused by uneven drying, gives the wood a cupped shape.

Cup shakes lead to splits along the grain line inside the wood.

Avoid selecting wood scraps with problems such as knots, splits, warping, and cup shakes. *From Lawrence 1979.*

Such lumber is called **rough sawn.** This lumber is usually put through a planer which smooths the board. Planed boards (dressed lumber) are easier and safer for young children to handle than rough sawn lumber, which can result in splinters. Children can compare the two types of boards and may want to see how much work is involved in sanding a rough board until it is smooth.

Defects. The more common defects that downgrade lumber are illustrated in Figure 3. **Knots** are very hard remains of branches. Clear wood does not have knots and is the best for children. Unfortunately it is usually expensive, so the most reasonable approach is to keep the number of knots as small as possible. Children soon learn about knots and how hard they are to saw or nail through.

Warping is usually caused by uneven drying and/or poor storage of the lumber. Boards warp or curve in three major ways, the concave part of the curve being the drier side of the board. A board which is **bowed** is curved along its face from end to end. A board which is **crooked** is curved along its edge from end to end. A board which is **cupped** is curved on its face from side to side. Cup warping is the most annoying to young children. Children can soak a piece of dry pine or fir in water to see how the grain rises, and how the wood warps. They can then put it in the sun to dry with a weight on top of the board to reverse the warping.

Splits or cracks, running with the grain, are a separation of the fibers. **Checks** are splits that are caused by uneven drying and usually occur on the ends of boards. **Shakes** are splits that may have occurred while the tree was growing, from damage in a wind storm, from lightning, from mistreatment by people, or from damage when the tree was felled. Shakes usually occur inside the wood along the grain, sometimes curved around the tree with the annual rings **(cup shakes),** sometimes filled with **pitch** (dried sap) and partly edged with bark where the tree had begun to heal itself. The latter are called **pitch shakes** or **pitch pockets** and should not be used by children.

Other wood products

Plywood. Plywood has been described as a wood sandwich (Adkins 1973) because it is made by gluing several layers of wood together with the grain of the layers at right angles. Plywood is thus very strong for spanning wide spaces. It comes in different grades and thicknesses as well as with different woods and glues. Plywood thicker than 12.5mm (1/2″) is not suggested for use with young children because it is heavy and hard to use. The 6.5mm (1/4″), 9.5mm (3/8″), and 12.5mm (1/2″) plywoods are lighter and easy to saw. Nailing into the edge of plywood does not hold and often causes splints, so plywood is not recommended for construction of boxes.

Wall boards. Other board products used in construction and insulation are fiberboard, hardboard (Masonite), and particleboard or chipboard. Fiberboard is sometimes recommended for use with young children because it is light, soft, and flexible. However, its flexibility often makes the saw bind, and because fiberboard breaks easily, it may be frustrating to use. Also, nails do not hold well so use in construction is not suggested. However, two-year-olds can hammer nails into it and pull them out again endlessly! Children who

Table 3.
Accessory materials.

Primary accessories	Secondary accessories
rope	watercolor markers
twine	thumb tacks
latex paints and brushes	tempera paints and brushes
glue	fabric and leather scraps
sandpaper	paper
tapes	vinyl strips
assorted pulleys, nuts, bolts,	innertubing
washers, sheet metal, metal	spools, jar lids
tubing, wire	cigar boxes
boiled linseed oil	fruit crates
1″ hinges with screws	tongue depressors, ice cream sticks
2″ hinges with screws	Styrofoam scraps
screw-eyes, assorted sizes	corks
1 1/2″ hooks and eyes	colored string and yarn
	rubber bands
	bottle caps

Note: Each teacher will have to decide whether to encourage young children to use bottle caps and other discards with woodworking. Some feel a love for wood and for the developing woodworking skills of children precludes introduction of discards, while others believe they enhance creative opportunities.

experience early success with woodworking will usually be confident about building on their skills as they grow. Due to the chemicals involved in processing these products, children should not be allowed to taste them.

Doweling. Doweling (machine-rounded sticks) can be purchased in different thicknesses. Teachers may want to keep a supply of 12.5mm (1/2″) and 25mm (1″) diameter doweling cut in meter lengths. Younger children sometimes use dowels as decoration. Older children create chimneys, handles, smoke stacks, towers, sailboat masts, and animal legs with dowels. Advanced woodworkers can use dowels as axles.

Accessory materials

Children can ingeniously use odds and ends such as those listed in Table 3. For more skilled children, provide a few small hinges with screws to match,

Figure 4. Wood dimensions

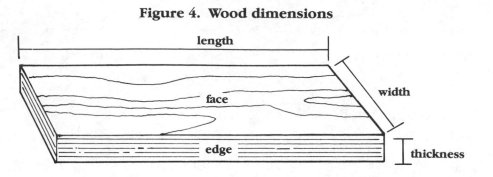

Lumber has three dimensions: thickness, width, and length.

From Cartwright 1975.

hooks and eyes, and screw-eyes of varied sizes. Hasps, metal shelf angles, and other such hardware may be bought as needed.

Wood sources

How do teachers find enough wood? Teachers or parents can ask for inexpensive or free scrap wood at building sites, lumber companies, and cabinet shops and usually get it. Remember to avoid too many pieces of hardwood such as yellow pine or oak. Discard boards with too many knots, splinters, and ragged edges as well as severely warped or cracked boards. Try to choose pieces in which the grain runs smoothly lengthwise and which are well seasoned. Kiln dried lumber is best.

Lumber is still sold in even-numbered feet, from 6' to 20' long. The change to metric dimensions for domestic sales has been delayed, but you can cut the boards you buy into 1m and 2m lengths to encourage metric measurement by children and to make convenient lengths for storage.

Soft white pine is by far the best wood to buy. Many lumber yards sell little other original wood except structural timber (heavy pieces) of fir and yellow pine. For white cedar and eastern spruce (good softwoods), and for walnut, oak, mahoganies, or teak, you may have to go to specialty outlets. Children will benefit from a well-planned shopping trip to purchase supplies. Lumber sizes are specified by three dimensions: thickness, width, and length, in that order (see Figure 4). For example, if you want a board 1" thick and 6" wide (25 x

150mm), and 8' long (2300mm), ask for a *one by six, eight feet long.* This is written 1" x 6"—8'. Note that these dimensions refer to rough sawn lumber. Dressed lumber, although it uses the rough sawn dimensions, is slightly smaller in thickness and width because of the planing needed to make it smooth. The dimensions of a dressed *one by six* are actually 3/4" x 5 1/2" (19 x 150mm).

It used to be possible to buy 1/2" lumber. However, it is easier for a beginner to nail into the edge of a 3/4" board than a 1/2" board without splitting. Two- to four-year-olds can manage well with plentiful and carefully selected scrap wood. Try to have on hand the following popular sizes for kindergarten through fifth grade:

White pine, nominal dimensions:

1" x 1"	1" x 4"
1" x 2"	1" x 6"
1" x 3"	1" x 8"

Hardwood doweling:

12.5mm (1/2") and 25mm (1") diameter

Fir plywood, interior grade, sanded both sides, in 4' x 8' sheets, which an adult or an older child can cut in metric measurement for convenient storage:

6.5mm (1/4") thick
9.5mm (3/8") thick
12.5mm (1/2") thick

Scrap wood, odd-sized pieces of pine, poplar, cedar, spruce, fir plywood, chipboard

Tools and accessories

Sturdy, small-scale adult tools are best. Toy tool kits and cheap tools will not do the job, and the cheapest tools may be the most expensive in the long run because they break easily (Osborn and Haupt 1964).

Workbench

A workbench should be about as high as the children's waists. It should be solid and sturdy enough to remain still while the child is hammering, shaping, or sawing. Workbenches may be purchased commercially but a heavy table, bench, or packing box can be converted into a woodworking bench. A smooth, flat, solid discarded door or heavy wood planks can be nailed to two sturdy boxes or sawhorses placed under either end. However, homemade workbenches must be strongly reinforced. A bottom shelf and/or drawers are nice for storage of wood or accessories but not necessary.

Figure 5. The sawing bench

Materials
1   1" x 6" #2 pine board, 8' long
1   2" x 10" fir plank, 26" long
    or 2   2" x 10" scraps at least 13" long
16 2½" headed nails

Tools
pencil
try square
saw
hammer

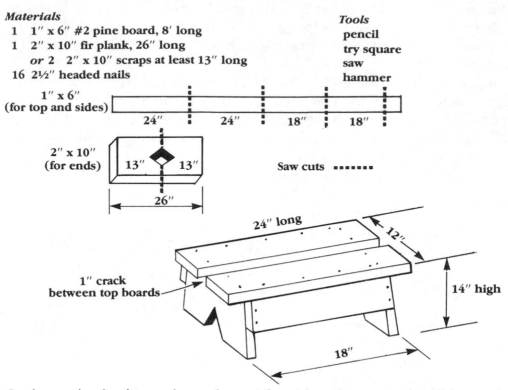

Cut the wood and nail it together as shown. A few nicks and uneven ends well fit a sturdy working saw bench!
From Cartwright 1975.

Sawing bench and nailing base

Children saw, hammer, shape, and sand their wood at a workbench using a vise to hold it, but workbenches are expensive. Children can also effectively clamp their wood to a low, less expensive, homemade sawing bench (see Figure 5 and photo on p. 21). The saw teeth cut on the downward push of the saw. The correct angle of about 45° for cutting is easily achieved at a sawing bench, but not at the workbench. When sawing at the saw bench, children should hold short boards with a clamp. They may hold long boards with their knee, their feet, or a clamp. Better still, a friend can sit on the wood, firmly holding it down to the saw bench. A sawing bench invites cooperation, while a workbench can foster disagreements or unsafe conditions if children use the vise or hammer too close to one another.

Children can clamp their wood to a low, inexpensive, homemade sawing bench. Using a vise or C-clamp to hold the wood while sawing, planing, or nailing makes woodworking much safer and easier.

Figure 6. Nailing base

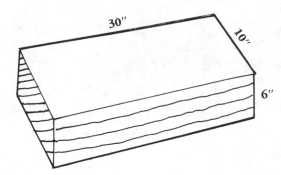

Use a heavy 6″ × 10″ timber to make a nailing base.
From Cartwright 1975.

The nailing base (see Figure 6) is also an inexpensive but excellent piece of equipment. Nailing is safer and surer when it is done on a firm and solid foundation. For a far quieter carpentry corner, children can hammer on a nailing base placed on a scrap of carpet rather than a resounding workbench. Noise at the workbench may be less if you use carpet under the legs of the bench.

A workbench is not necessary to have a successful carpentry area. Instead use one or more sawing benches and solid, heavy nailing bases, as they can be more easily moved, are less noisy, and take less room than the large workbench. If you already have a suitable workbench and space for it, by all means use it, but you might want to try the sawing bench and nailing base as well.

Vise or C-clamp

Most commercial workbenches are equipped with a vise to hold wood steady for shaping, not sawing. If a vise is not available, large C-clamps shaped like the letter *C* (100–150mm [4″–6″] opening) will do nearly the same job. A vise or C-clamp should be placed at the end of the table—on opposite sides when two are used per table, so children will have enough space to work. Using a vise or C-clamp to hold the wood while filing, planing, or nailing often makes woodworking safer and easier.

Hammers

Well-balanced steel-shanked claw hammers (7 to 13 ounces in weight) are best (see Figure 7). When the hammer is too light, the nail won't go into the wood. If it is too heavy, the hand must be held too close to the head, which is

Figure 7. Claw hammers

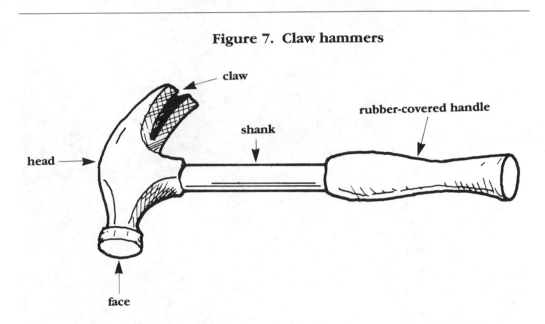

The steel-shanked hammer comes in many sizes and invites the child to hold it correctly.

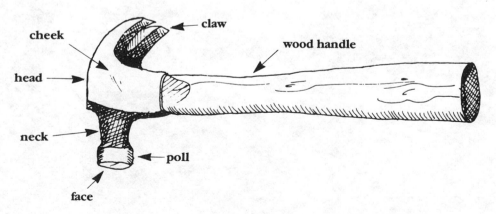

A well-balanced claw hammer is best for beginners (From Blackburn 1977).

For maximum leverage and power the hammer should be held toward the back of the handle. A light, well-balanced steel-shanked hammer is ideal for young children.

Figure 8. Crowbars

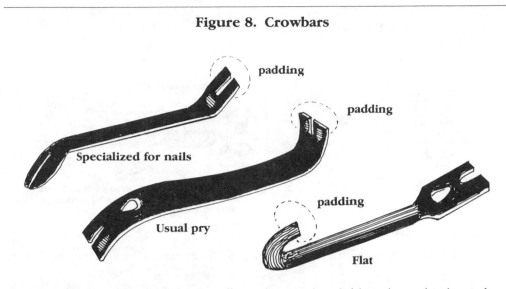

It is best to pad the handle ends of small crowbars so that children do not hit themselves in the face when the nail suddenly comes out. The crowbar is so named because of the *crow's foot* on the end.

called *choking,* and the nail usually bends over while the child's aim waivers with fatigue. For maximum leverage and power the hammer should be held toward the back end of the handle (see photo on p. 24). Woodworking beginners often choke the hammer to get better control, but as skill is gained the child should be encouraged to move the hand away from the hammer head.

One of the most satisfying ways for children of any age to learn to hammer is simply to pound nails into a well-cut tree stump (see photo on p. 56). An older child or the teacher may start a roofing nail, with a large head, for a two-year-old, so that a child will not need to put fingers near the nail to be pounded. But most children aged three years and older can start their own roofing nails (the large head protects fingers) and derive much satisfaction from the process. It is a fine way to let off steam as well as gain nailing skill. Three-year-olds and older children can pull out the nails again, but they should use a nail-pulling device with a padded end (see Figure 8) for best results, because the claws on lightweight hammers are often too thick and the leverage too short (see photo on p. 56). Driving nails into the end grain of the stump is far easier than cross-grain nailing. Children use old nail holes to start their nails, thus achieving the whole operation with gratifying independence.

Figure 9. Tightening a loose hammer head

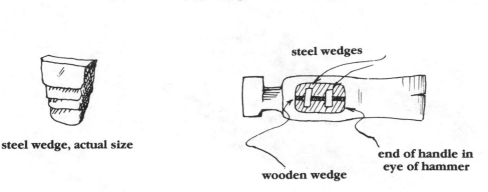

steel wedge, actual size

steel wedges

end of handle in eye of hammer

wooden wedge

Drive small steel wedges into the eye of the hammer to tighten the head (From Blackburn 1977).

Be sure to keep hammers in good repair. For example, a chipped face is extremely dangerous and the hammer should be thrown away. Similarly, hammer heads of wood-handled hammers may come loose and hit someone. A hammer head can be tightened by pounding small steel wedges into the eye of the hammer (see Figure 9). Broken, split, or cracked handles can pinch or bruise and should be replaced, not repaired. To avoid these problems we suggest buying steel-shanked hammers whose heads are welded to their handles.

Nails

The nail should match the child's purpose and skill. Provide nails with large-sized heads for beginners—roofing, wire, and box nails are best (see Figure 10). Nails with small heads like casing and finishing nails can be introduced to children as they become more experienced.

To start a nail, hold it in place with one hand and tap lightly with the hammer. When the nail stands firmly by itself, remove your hand and hit the nail with strong strokes of the hammer. If the nail does not go in properly, remove it.

To remove a nail with a claw hammer, hold the wood or clamp it down, slip the claws of the hammer under the nail head, and pull the handle back toward

Figure 10. Types of nails

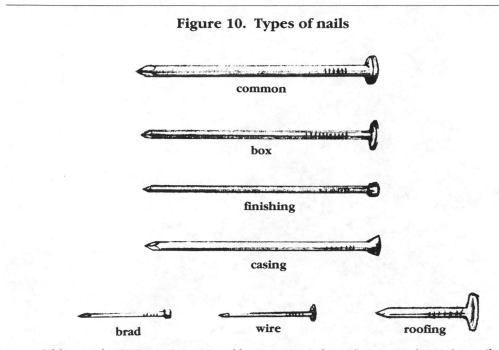

common

box

finishing

casing

brad   wire   roofing

From Gilden et al. 1977, p. 15. Reprinted by permission from the National 4-H Council.

you until the head of the nail is about an inch out of the wood. Then place a block of wood under the hammer head to make it easier to pull the nail out and to protect the wood from dents (see photo on p. 28). Pull the end of the handle slowly toward you.

Children will have fewer nails to remove if you help them select the proper size nail (see Figure 11). To measure for the nail, position the wood in its finished position. Hold the nail to the side of the wood. Usually a nail should go no more than two-thirds of the way into the lower of the two pieces of wood after they are nailed together (see photo on p. 30). Longer nails may split the wood or go into the workbench or nailing base. Shorter ones will not hold the wood together. In most cases, nail the thinner piece of wood to the thicker one so it will hold better.

Start all nails in the top piece of wood, driving them in until their points just show through the bottom side. Place this piece on the thicker piece exactly where you want it with both pieces firmly held on the nailing base. Then finish hammering the nail through. If it is tricky to hold both pieces of wood in the correct position, tap one or two nails (that are already through the top piece)

Placing a block of wood under the hammer head makes it easier to pull the nail out and protects the wood from dents.

Figure 11. Common nail sizes

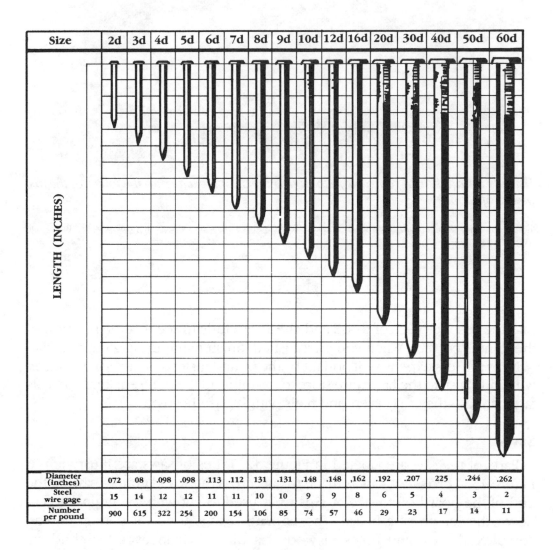

The Incredible Illustrated Tool Book, Copyright © 1974 by Pathfinder Publications, Inc., Division of Arrow Publishing Co., Inc., Canton, MA 02021. Reproduced with permission of the Copyright owner.

Usually a nail should go no more than two-thirds of the way into the lower of the two pieces of wood.

Photograph from *Woodworking for Kids,* by Frank D. Torre. © 1978 by Frank D. Torre. Reprinted by permission of Doubleday & Company, Inc.

into the second piece of wood and check carefully to see that the position of the joint is correct. When you are satisfied, finish hammering all the nails.

Nails are less expensive if bought by the pound instead of the box. Children will find a visit to the hardware store to examine all the different kinds of nails fascinating—they may even find nails with square heads!

Saws

Parts of the saw are labeled in Figure 12. Types of saws are illustrated in Figure 13. A **crosscut saw** is made to cut across the wood grain—sawing the end of the board off to size. A **ripsaw** is used to cut with the grain—to cut down the length of a board. The **coping saw** is used for cutting curves, complex shapes, and holes in wood—a difficult maneuver for children. Blades for the coping saw come in fine, medium, and coarse (which refers to the spacing and depth of the teeth) and are interchangeable. Blades should be 3.2mm (1/8″) to 6.5mm (1/4″) thick. A coping saw is usually best used with children at least eight years old.

The **keyhole** or **compass saw** is light and easy for young children to handle. It can also be used for sawing in tight places, cutting slightly rounded curves, or other openings. Bore a hole with a 19mm (3/4″) bit to start the saw on an inside cut in the middle of a piece of wood. With close supervision, a two-year-old can use this small, yet strong-bladed saw. You can buy a keyhole saw with different size blades that attach to the handle with wingnuts. Unlike the larger crosscut saws and ripsaws, coping and keyhole saws may be used at a workbench with the wood held in a vise.

A 400mm to 500mm (16″ to 20″) crosscut saw is best for most young children. A 10 point saw is recommended—the *10* means there are 10 teeth per inch. Buy strong, good quality steel since the teeth of the saw may bend when poor quality is used and/or soon become dull.

Like hammering, sawing is a basic skill every woodworker must learn. As with many other skills, practice is essential. Before beginning to saw, select the wood and mark the place to be sawed with a pencil line. Either clamp or put the wood in the vise so the part to be sawed extends past the end of the table.

Figure 12. Parts of a hand saw

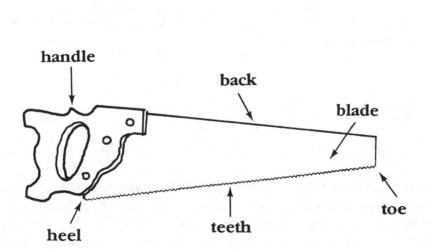

From Gilden et al. 1975, p. 12. Reprinted by permission from the National 4-H Council.

Figure 13. Types of saws and blades

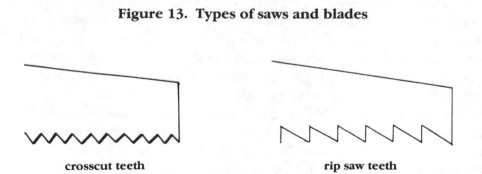

crosscut teeth   rip saw teeth

Crosscut and rip saws are distinguished by the shape of their teeth.

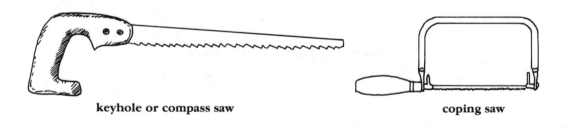

keyhole or compass saw   coping saw

Otherwise use the low sawing bench. Place the part to be sawed as close to the vise or clamp as possible to avoid slipping or vibration during the pressure of sawing. Start the cut on the side of the line *away* from the piece you plan to use because the sawing removes about 3mm from the lengthwise measurement of the wood in the form of sawdust. Gently pull the saw toward you, starting a groove. Use your thumbnail to keep the saw by the line only while drawing the saw toward you. The groove will help hold the saw in place. Then begin to saw in the forward direction with the saw held at a 40° to 50° angle. On the forward, more forceful downstroke you will be cutting the wood. Ease off while pulling on the upstroke.

Before using wood, two-year-old children or other beginners can try saw-

Figure 14. Hand drill

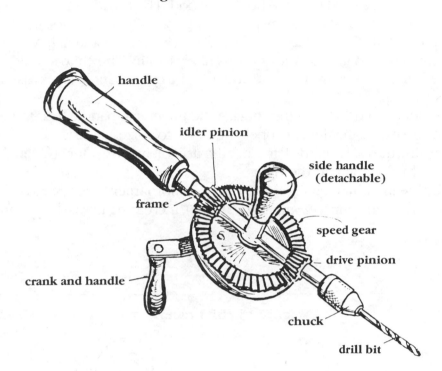

From Gilden et al. 1975, p. 13. Reprinted by permission from the National 4-H Council.

ing Styrofoam or soft fiberboard, as long as it does not bend and bind the saw. Soap can be put on the saw blade to prevent friction.

You will get better use of the saw with proper maintenance. Occasionally wipe the saw with a lightweight machine oil after use to prevent rust. Any accumulation of dirt, dust, or grease should be carefully wiped away before oiling. Saws should be hung up when not in use and oiled when they must be stored for long periods like summer vacation. If saws are used frequently, sharpen them once or twice a year as needed. Rusted saws can be rejuvenated by sanding or rubbing with steel wool and antirust oil. Rub wooden parts of all tools with a small amount of linseed oil every two or three years. The oil helps preserve the wood and its appearance.

Boring tools

Boring tools are used to make holes in wood. The **hand drill** (see Figure 14) is used to drill small holes like guide holes for nails and screws. It is easier to start the drill if a small hole is first made with a hammer and nail. When the drill point is placed in this hole, it is less likely to slip. The child should then hold the drill handle with one hand and turn the crank handle clockwise with the other hand.

When putting a drill bit in the chuck, hold the crank, handle, and frame in one hand. Use the other hand to open the chuck to a size a little larger than the bit by turning the chuck to the left. Place the drill bit in the center and retighten the chuck by turning it to the right.

The **brace and bit** (see Figure 15) are used for larger holes. Standard bits are available from 6mm to 25mm (1/4″ to 1″), increasing in size by 1.5mm or

Figure 15. Bit brace

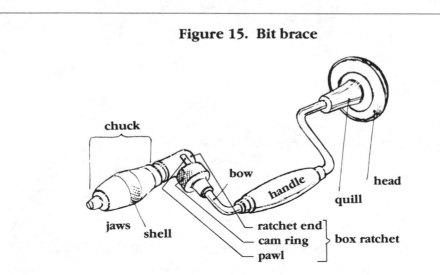

From Gilden et al. 1975, p. 14. Reprinted by permission from the National 4-H Council.

1/16". A rachet allows you to drill holes where space is limited. When inserting the bit into the brace chuck, first hold the chuck. Then turn the handle clockwise until the jaws are open. Put the long end of the bit into the open jaw. Turn the handle counterclockwise until the jaws are tight, making sure the bit is straight.

All boring tools are difficult to use and are not recommended until children have had a great deal of experience doing woodworking. Fine motor activities such as using snap clothespins, an egg beater, or scissors are good preparatory activities before using boring tools. Many children will need the teacher to hold the tool steady and straight while they turn it which is a good reason not to introduce boring tools early. Children can learn to manipulate the brace and bit by first placing the wood in the vise. The bit is then placed against the wood. The child leans against the handle, holding it firmly against her or his chest. Leaning on the brace in this way makes the bit cut into the wood. The hand drill can be used from the side in a similar manner. It is important to turn the gear handle at a steady rate and hold the drill straight. If the drill is crooked, it may snap the bit off. In any case, always keep hands away from the turning bit. A child may also practice drilling scrap wood on the floor, while kneeling on the wood to hold it firmly. A second piece of wood may be placed below the drilled wood to protect the floor.

Screwdrivers and screws

Screwdrivers are dangerous. They are best used only by children with advanced coordination and skill. You can get a bad cut if the point slips. Use a vise or clamp to hold the project firmly. A good rule to follow is this: as with a knife or saw or chisel, never get any part of your body in front of the screwdriver.

There are two types of screwdrivers—standard and Phillips (see Figure 16). The tip of the standard screwdriver is flat and is used with screw heads that have straight slots. A Phillips screwdriver is needed for screws with cross-shaped slots. Screwdrivers come in a variety of sizes. The tip of the screwdriver should be the same width as the slot and fit securely in the slot. A screwdriver tip that is too narrow, worn, or damaged will slip out of the screw slot. A worn screwdriver tip should be reground or replaced.

To use the screwdriver, start a hole for the screw with a nail or drill. Applying soap to the screw makes driving it easier. For the first few turns only, hold the screw between the thumb and forefinger to steady it. Use the screwdriver very gently while your fingers are nearby! Turn the screw into the wood until the two pieces are well joined and the screw is tight.

All boring tools are difficult to use and are not recommended until children have had a great deal of experience doing woodworking.

Figure 16. Screwdriver

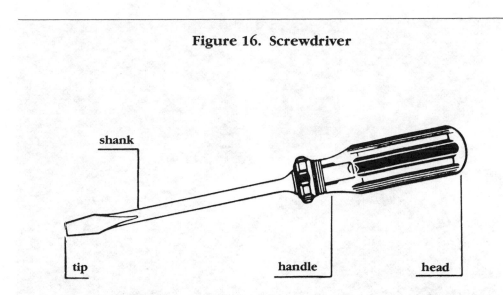

From Gilden et al. 1973, p. 12. Reprinted by permission from the National 4-H Council.

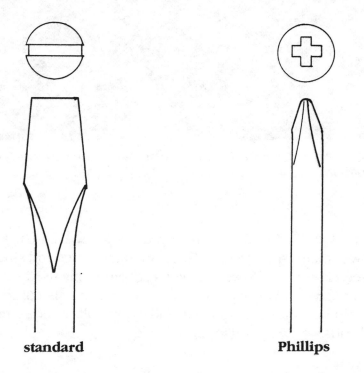

standard   **Phillips**

The width, thickness, and shape of the tip of a screwdriver are very important.

Screws are used in woodworking because a screw's threads have more holding power than a smooth nail.

Screws are used in woodworking because a screw's threads have more holding power than a smooth nail. There are many types and sizes of screws available (see Figure 17). However, the most commonly used wood screw is the **flat head screw.** Many types of bolts and nuts are also used with wood when the child becomes experienced, and many bolts need screwdrivers to hold their heads.

Shaping tools

Sure Forms. The Sure Form is safe and easier to use than either files or planes when the child wants to smooth rough or uneven saw cuts and make rounded corners or bevelled edges. As seen in Figure 18, Sure Forms, made by Stanley tools, come in flat, semiround, or fully rounded (rattail) types or in block-plane types. Their multibladed surface is used like a file and cuts as cleanly and smoothly as a plane but with far more ease, control, and swiftness. Children ages three years and older can use this simple tool with immediate satisfaction. Two or three types of Sure Forms are the only shaping tools required for young children. However, like the workbench, wood files, rasps, and block planes are traditional tools which children and adults like to learn to use as they become experienced. They are therefore described here.

Figure 17. Screws

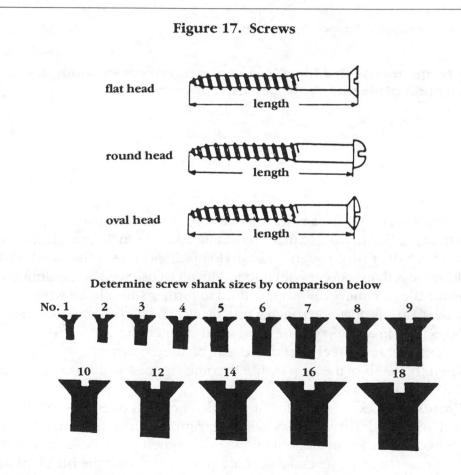

Determine screw shank sizes by comparison below

From Gilden et al. 1975, p. 16. Reprinted by permission from the National 4-H Council.

Figure 18. Sure Forms

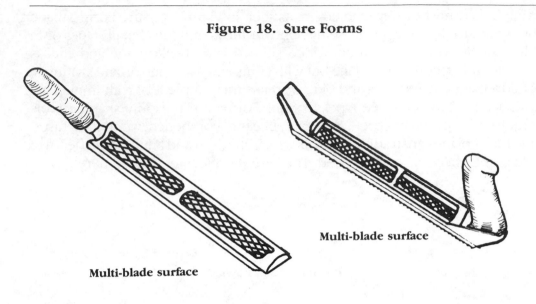

Multi-blade surface

Multi-blade surface

Multi-blade surface

Sure Forms are handled like files and planes, but cut smoothly and easily with a multi-blade surface. Blades are replaceable.

Filing tools. A **wood rasp** is like a very rough and giant fingernail file. Like the Sure Form, it is useful for rounding edges or making a rough saw cut more even. The rasp is rough, and hard to hold, and slower than a Sure Form. Children less than six years old find it difficult to use well. A medium coarse **cabinet file,** 250mm (10″) can be used to further smooth the wood surface after the rasp has done the rough work. Using two hands is necessary, and the wood is held in a clamp or vise. Rasps and cabinet files are for use on wood only. A special hard steel **metal file** may be used on metal.

When the teeth of the rasp or file become clogged with wood dust, clean with a stiff wire brush.

Planes. Planes are good for fine work when you need to even, level, or smooth the wood. They are also useful for trimming the edge of a board down to desired size when the amount of wood trimmed off the edge is not more than 16mm. There are several different types of planes but the **block plane** is the most practical for the young woodworker. A 150mm to 175mm (6″ to 7″)

block plane (see Figure 19) can be introduced to children who have developed sufficient coordination skills. A Sure Form is better for children less coordinated and skilled. First, help the child draw a line the length of the board to show the depth to which the child is going to plane. Make sure that the wood to be smoothed is placed in the vise and that the child has both hands on the plane. The child should make smooth, even strokes in one direction, with the grain. If the planed surface feels rough, stroke the plane in the opposite direction and the wood will be clean and smooth. It is a joy to cut curling wood shavings with a plane. But never plane over nails, because the blade of the plane can be damaged easily.

To insert the cutting blade into the plane, put the blade in **with the bevelled side up.** Then put the lever cap in position and tighten the lever cap screw. The blade should project through the bottom of the plane evenly,

Figure 19. Block plane

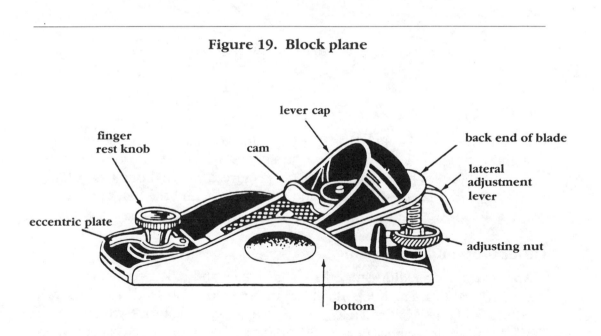

The block plane is used with the bevel side of the blade up.

From Gilden et al. 1973, p. 13. Reprinted by permission from the National 4-H Council.

Figure 20. How to adjust a blade in a block plane

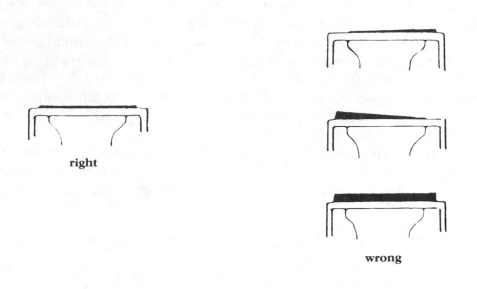

right

wrong

From Gilden et al. 1973, p. 15. Reprinted by permission from the National 4-H Council.

poking through at about the thickness of thin cardboard. To make the blade straight, loosen the lever cap screw, straighten the blade, and retighten the screw. To adjust for thickness of blade (see Figure 20), turn the adjusting knob to the right to push the blade out and to the left to pull the blade in.

Other tools and equipment

Sandpaper. Sanding smooths rough edges and sides, particularly saw cuts across the grain. Keep on hand three grades of sandpaper: coarse, medium, and fine. Children may choose to use a sanding block, which can be made by wrapping sandpaper tightly on a scrap block of wood. Except when sanding board ends, sand back and forth in the same direction as the wood grain, not across the grain, to avoid scratch marks.

Glue. Glue is useful for joining pieces of wood together, holding decoration, and repairing accidentally split wood. Teachers may want to keep a tube

Sand back and forth in the same direction as the wood grain to avoid scratch marks.

of *quick drying glue,* such as Duco cement, to use with care for small projects. White glue, such as Elmer's, can be used for most projects. Waterproof glues should always be used with objects that will be outdoors. Children can use clamps, a vise, or weights (for example, bricks) to hold the pieces of wood under pressure until the glue dries.

Safety goggles. Children can wear safety goggles when they are working with wood in order to protect their eyes from flying wood chips or sawdust, but goggles often hamper vision and may themselves cause accidents. Teachers who are careful about safety often prefer not to use goggles. However, many child care centers' policies and some regulations insist on their use, so if you are required to use goggles, buy the unbreakable plastic wraparound style with air vents to prevent fogging, which permits fairly good vision.

Miscellaneous items. Some other tools and equipment teachers may keep on hand are listed here.

pliers	try square (see Figure 24)
metric ruler	chalk
tinsnips	awl
wire cutters	dust pan
petroleum jelly	small broom or brush

Metric system

The world is well on its way to measuring by metrics. Woodworking provides a wonderful opportunity for parents, teachers, and children to use the metric system. Adults can buy a meter stick (see Figure 21) rather than a

---

Figure 21. Metric/inches ruler

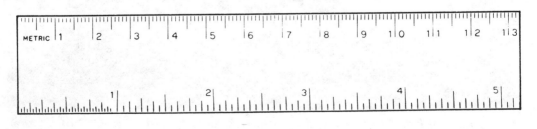

Table 4.
Metric conversion table.

Inches	Millimeters	Inches	Millimeters
1/16	1.5	16	405
1/8	3	17	430
1/4	6	18	455
1/2	12.5	19	480
5/8	16	20	505
3/4	19	21	530
7/8	22	22	555
1	25	23	580
2	50	24	610
3	75	25	635
4	100	26	660
5	125	27	685
6	150	28	710
7	175	29	735
8	200	30	760
9	225	31	785
10	250	32	810
11	275	33	835
12	305	34	860
13	330	35	885
14	355	36	915
15	380		

yardstick for children's use and provide rulers that have a metric scale. Metric measurements can be made by older five-year-olds especially when the children are purposely involved. However, it is likely to be some years before we are able to buy wood cut according to metric measurement. Children learn metrics best by their own firsthand experience with measuring and estimating until they can visualize centimeters and meters. Conversion tables (see Table 4) should only be used by adults until they become familiar with metric measurements.

CHAPTER 3

Setting Up the Woodworking Center

Several factors need to be considered before a woodworking center is set up. Woodworking should be in a separate area free from distractions. Children running by can be accidentally hit or cause the woodworker to be hurt. Also, frustration can increase when too much activity distracts the woodworker. Woodworking is filled with the noise of purposeful hard work which is one of the reasons children enjoy it so much. But when this noice distracts others, it can be lessened by careful placement of the woodworking area as well as sound-proofing techniques.

The bench and workspace require considerable room, and the number of children using the area must be limited to ensure that children can work without interfering with each other (see Chapter 4). For these reasons you may not want to set up in your classroom unless you have ample space and can soften the noise. Consider setting up your woodworking area in an empty room, in a hallway, outdoors, or in any secluded area out of the way of traffic flow. Placing the woodworking center in a corner helps because distractions can come from only two directions. However, the woodworking center should not be so isolated that children feel cut off from everyone else or do not have reasonable access to other learning activities—constructed items can often be incorporated in dramatic play, for example.

Tools and wood should be stored near the work area. Remember that wood is flammable. Keep only dry wood—carefully wipe wet or oily pieces before storage. Wood scraps can be stored in baskets, boxes, or wooden bins. Clear strong plastic containers, open cans, and child-made wooden boxes which may fit in shelves are good for storing nails and other accessories. Glass containers should seldom be used with young children because they break too easily. (Many carpenters prefer glass jars for small screws and nails.) Different types of nails and other materials can be sorted by the children into separate containers. Tape or staple the appropriate item on the outside of each

*A woodworking center in a classroom requires ample
space and can be very noisy. Consider setting up your
woodworking area in an empty room, a hallway, outdoors, or any secluded area out of the traffic flow.*

container with name and metric size written as well to facilitate locating and sorting. Children enjoy using a large magnet to gather stray nails during cleanup.

As shown in Figure 22, a tool rack can be made using plywood or 19mm (3/4″) boards held together with 1″ x 2″ straps across the back. Screw-in hooks or nails can hold the tools. Outline the tools on the board with a marker to enable children to put away tools independently (see photo on p. 50). Reading skills can be encouraged when the name or a picture of the tool is

Tools and wood should be stored near the work area.

Outline the tools on the board to enable children to put away tools independently.

placed under each outline. Do not use perforated Masonite with hooks to hold tools. The holes become enlarged, hooks fall out and get lost, and Masonite holds tools very poorly.

Sometimes it is helpful if the tool rack is portable so tools can be used temporarily in another location or stored out of reach. Depending on public access to the classroom a wall-mounted tool rack that can be closed and locked may be necessary. Two types of locking cabinets are suggested in Figure 22.

Commercial versions of these storage racks are available but should be evaluated before purchase to ensure that they will be appropriate for use with your tools.

Tool boxes are inappropriate for storing tools, as tools can be damaged easily and children or adults can cut themselves while searching for the proper tool.

Figure 22. Tool storage

Tool rack

30″

¾″ wide

48″

pencils

bits

From Cartwright 1975, p. 3. Reprinted by permission from the author.

Locking tool cabinet

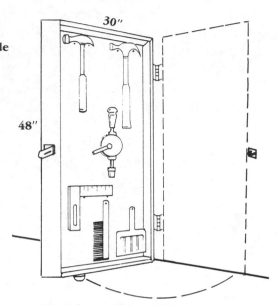

30″

48″

To make a locking cabinet, screw a 1″ x 6″ pine border around a plywood backing. Hinge on one side. Turn this cabinet to the wall and lock in place with a hasp and a padlock.

From Cartwright 1975, p. 4. Reprinted by permission from the author.

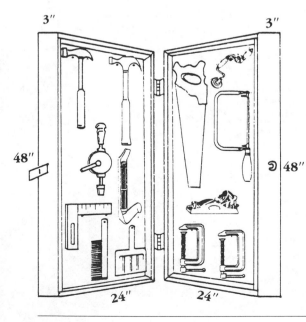

3″   3″

48″   48″

24″   24″

Folding tool cabinet

Screw 1″ x 3″ pine to the plywood backing. Hinge both sections together and lock with a hasp and padlock.

From Cartwright 1975, p. 4. Reprinted by permission from the author.

CHAPTER 4

Working with Children

A young teacher reported, "I decided to set up the woodworking center outside. It was such a sunny day and I thought we would all enjoy being out and it wouldn't be so noisy. I laid out all the hammers, saws, files, brace and bit, and the plane. And I put out a good assortment of nails and materials for decoration. My set up was beautiful! (Or so I thought.) Everyone would have a great time. Well, everyone probably did have a good time, but not the kind of time I had envisioned. As I surveyed the damage, I wondered what had gone wrong. It started well enough. But soon the workbench was crowded and children got angry. I was barely able to stop Matthew before he hit Jenny's fingers with the hammer. And before I knew it, the workbench was full of nails and had a huge gash made with the saw. The safety goggles disappeared into the sand box, and one hammer still has not been found. The children pounded several dents in the water table and started making guns out of the hammers. How could all of this happen in just ten minutes? Fortunately, I was able to call a halt and put away all the woodworking equipment before anyone was physically hurt. There must be more to know about woodworking than just how to buy and use equipment, I thought as I retrieved the last piece of wood from under a nearby bush."

Indeed there is more to know about woodworking with young children than how to select, use, and care for tools. The teacher's attitude and role in planning and organizing the learning experience such as setting up the woodworking center, matching activities to developmental abilities of children, and providing guidance are essential if woodworking activities with young children are to be safe, positive learning experiences.

Young children are very quick to feel your uncertainties or fears about woodwork and the use of sharp or heavy tools. Their reactions may surface in shyness, acting out, poor coordination, or recklessness. It is critical that you practice with tools until you feel assured and competent. In the home or classroom, the tone created by the parent or teacher is an important, pervasive part of the learning situation. Your genuine respect for children's capacities

The teacher's attitude and role in organizing the learning experience such as setting up the woodworking center, matching activities to developmental abilities of children, and providing guidance are essential if woodworking activities with young children are to be safe, positive learning experiences.

and limitations, for their curiosity and initiative, for their innate desire to learn well, needs to come through clearly in your daily relations with them. Teacher-child relations in woodworking are no exception.

Introducing woodworking activities

The woodworking abilities and interests of young children vary greatly from child to child and at different ages. Some children love to do woodworking often while others enjoy it less frequently. Some become quite skilled while others have more difficulty. However, children do go through a fairly ordered sequence of stages in woodworking (Brandhofer 1971; Moffitt 1973).

In the first stage, as long as adults do not set goals, children are *interested in process* (see photo on p. 56). They are not interested in making a product such as a boat or birdhouse, although they may label a piece of wood by such names. Instead, they use all their senses to explore the equipment and supplies. For example, two-year-old Brad loves to stack and unstack the wood. He is involved in the process of feeling, smelling, tasting, and moving the wood around. He is curious about the material. When Brad is three, he will probably pound nails and saw wood just for the fun of increasing his skill, of mastery, and building his self-esteem. He will enjoy making sawdust by sawing across the grain. He will put his whole body into the effort and need space and time in which to work at his own varying pace toward his own ends.

In the next stage, four-year-olds like Brad are likely to experiment with *combining* pieces—gluing and nailing. Soon the form of the children's work will remind them of a boat or other object and they will name it. But it is not until Brad has satisfied his curiosity and developed beginning skills in using wood and tools that he will become really interested in having a product—a specific object. Then at about age five Brad gradually enters the *product stage* and now wants to make a boat. In this stage, although the interest and pleasure in *process* should never die, children have an idea of a product in mind before beginning. At first the idea is usually changed, may be forgotten, or may not be finished. But as children become more experienced, skilled, and mature, they make finished products which are increasingly complex and realistic (see photo on p. 57).

As mentioned before, children at the same age may have vastly different skills in woodworking. In fact each child's skill, interest, and frustration level varies hourly, depending on a host of personal and situational factors (Cartwright 1982). Brad is a typical preschooler with good experiences in woodworking. Other children's pacing would be different, and many might not advance beyond the exploratory and skill building stage of driving nails into wood during the preschool years.

In the first stage of creative woodworking, children are interested in process. They are not interested in making a product. In the second stage children experiment with combining pieces.

As children become more experienced, skilled, and mature, they make finished products that are increasingly complex and realistic.

In addition to woodworking, several related activities might interest children and introduce them to other ideas. For example, children with limited skills may enjoy making sculptures with wood, sawdust, and glue, or they may want to sand or paint wood. Reading *The Toolbox, Building a House,* or other books could expand children's knowledge about tools and woodworking (see the Annotated Bibliography for suggestions). Flannelboard figures and stories, colorful pictures of tools, and other similar items may spark children's interest. You may want to invite a resource person such as a carpenter or industrial arts teacher to visit your program and build with the children. Field trips to a cabinet shop or repeated visits to a construction site will give children a better understanding of how woodworking is an integral part of our lives. Children may want to dictate stories, draw, or otherwise record their experiences.

When a child seems ready to use tools, introduce one tool at a time. Give the child an opportunity to handle the tool. Talk about how the tool is to be used before woodworking begins. The teacher will also need to demonstrate use of the tool. A hammer is not only dramatic but also a fairly easy tool for a child to use so introduce it first. As previously mentioned, a good tree stump, or log section 12″ long, is great for hammering practice. The nailing block, bench,

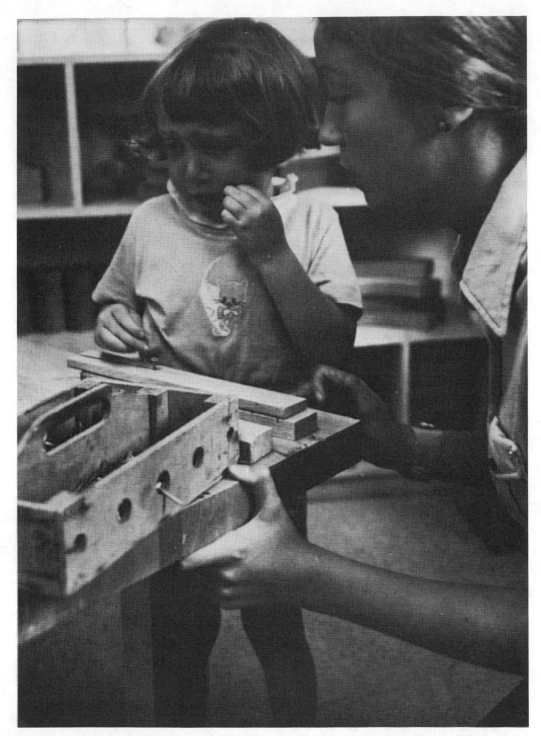

During woodworking the teacher can observe children for signs of fatigue or frustration to determine when to offer help.

vise, and/or C-clamp can be introduced next so the child will have opportunities to join pieces of wood together. Introduce the saw after the child is able to use a hammer with some degree of competence. As a child becomes more skilled in woodworking, you can introduce some of the more complex hand tools. Electric power tools should not be introduced until a child reaches full mastery of hand tools so that the child stays close to the material in feeling, skill, and depth of understanding. Tools can also be dangerous if introduced before children are ready or without proper supervision. Accessory materials may be added by the children as they become interested in making a product.

Support for children

Brian, hammering, misses the nail. "Stupid head!" taunts Lisa. Brian's face reddens. He raises his hammer to threaten Lisa.

To avoid such potentially dangerous and explosive situations at the workbench the teacher should allow children their own choice of workmates. They will choose their friends and seldom fight.

During woodworking the teacher can observe children for signs of fatigue or frustration to determine when to offer help. If the child is tired the teacher may suggest a break, offering to hold the materials the child has selected until a better time. The teacher may need to help start the nail after the child has determined where the nail should go. Removing a bent nail sometimes requires help, especially from another child. If necessary, assist the child in selecting nails that will not go through the wood and stick into the bench, but help just enough so children can finish by themselves. When the teacher does all the work, children learn very little and are robbed of a feeling of accomplishment and belief in their own ability.

If the project seems to be one which stretches their abilities, help children think through their ideas. Ask questions designed to stimulate problem solving:

"What could you use for legs on your table? How can you brace them? What will happen if they are not all the same length?"

"How far will this nail go into the bottom board?"

"What do you think is the most important thing about a boat?"

"What else do you need?"

"How can you put the wheels on your car?"

Since even five-year-olds concentrate on process more than product, do not be upset if plans are not carried out or work is not completed to your expectations. To insist that everything must be completed and done according to your standards robs children of opportunities for creativity and may kill their interest in woodworking.

The teacher's genuine appreciation during and after woodworking is done encourages further woodworking and builds positive relations as teacher and child share in the happiness of the experience. Instead of insulting a child by asking "What is it?" try comments such as "Tell me about what you've made."

The teacher also has a good opportunity to encourage social and emotional development through woodworking activities. For example, when plenty of materials are provided and woodworking is readily available, children have their own needs met and feel freer to share, help each other, and patiently wait their turn. When the teacher indicates pride in their helping, sharing, or patience, such behavior increases.

Young children's cognitive development does not enable them to understand the danger of using tools, but if proper tools are used in a well-planned environment where there is sensitive, direct adult supervision, woodworking can be a very safe activity.

Teachers can increase the likelihood that the child with fewer skills will learn from another child if teachers praise social behavior. For example, "Niko, that was nice of you to let Elizabeth use some of your nails." Or "Christine, your idea to use a longer piece of wood on Michael's house really helped him." Comments like "Michael is building such a nice house, why can't you do that well?" or "Look how fast Michael is nailing" just foster competition—not helping behavior. Christine's feelings about herself are certainly not enhanced, and Michael concentrates on speed instead of accuracy and safety.

Negative as well as positive situations can be guided to help children feel better about themselves and develop better social skills. For example, teachers can make it clear that they cannot accept behaviors such as ridicule, misuse of tools, or interference with someone else's work. However, teachers can avoid shaming or condemning the child by indicating that the behavior, not the child, is unacceptable. For example, "I know you saw well, but I can't let you saw on Jeff's wood." The teacher might also put an arm around the child's shoulder and gently remove the child from the workbench.

Teachers can also encourage children to talk about how they feel about such problems, why they acted as they did, why others behaved as they did, and how the problem could have been resolved more successfully (see Stone 1978). In the beginning children may be unable or unwilling to express feelings. Sometimes children can talk to puppets or dictate a story when they cannot talk to the teacher. Or they may not be ready to do anything. The teacher can say "I understand" and patiently wait. If the teacher tries to force children to talk out their concerns by demanding that they talk or by putting words into their mouths, children will become resentful and rebellious. But with opportunity, love, and understanding most children will eventually open up and take a more active part in building their socioemotional relationships.

Safety

Young children from ages two through four are just developing eye-hand and gross motor coordination. Their level of cognitive development does not enable them to automatically understand the danger of using tools, but if proper tools are used in a well-planned environment where there is sensitive, direct adult supervision, woodworking can be a safe activity. We have already discussed the selection, use, and care of good tools and the general role of the teacher. In this section we will concentrate on the immediate environment.

When children are beginning to do woodworking or lack self-control, it is best to have only one or two children at the workbench at a time. Children can work on each side of the bench at opposite ends. Materials should be readily available so that children do not get into each other's way. The use of a saw bench is another safety feature (see Figure 5).

Tools must be kept in good repair. More accidents are caused by dull tools than by those with sharp blades. The sharp saw is able to do the job with minimum effort, but a dull saw may slip, causing injury or frustration. Loose handles on hammers and saws may cause accidents, too. Become familiar with the recommendations on care of tools outlined in Chapter 2 so you can prevent needless injury to yourself or a child.

First aid

When splinters, cuts, or scratches occur, treat them immediately, no matter how small, to avoid infection and soothe feelings. When a child gets a serious splinter, remove it with tweezers if it is not too deeply embedded. Then wash the area well with soap and water. You may wish to check your records to make sure the child has had an up-to-date tetanus shot especially if the child has been working with barnyard wood. If the splinter is deeply embedded or a piece of it is left in the skin, the child may need medical attention. For a scratch or a small cut, wash the area well with soap and water and cover with a bandage. If the child has a major open wound, stop the bleeding by putting clean gauze pads on it and applying pressure. Then obtain medical assistance. If a child has been hit with a hammer there may be some discoloration or swelling. Run cold water over or apply ice to the area to reduce pain. If the skin is broken, if there is a possibility of damage to the bone, if the fingernail is discolored or warm to the touch, or if the child is in continued pain, seek medical help, preferably the child's personal physician. When any injury to a child occurs, notify the parent or guardian.

Teachers can help children understand not only woodworking but its *safety* by providing opportunities for the child to learn by doing. For example, encourage the child to gently feel the sharp teeth of the saw, the point of a bit, and the weight of a hammer, and ask what would happen if we misused the tools.

Specific safety limits

1. Tools are to be used only when an adult supervises.
2. No more than two children should be at the workbench at a time. Children who are observing should stand well away from the area. A crowded work area can contribute to accidents.
3. The work area should be kept free from clutter—with only the materials in direct use in the area. Hardware, glue, and accessories should be stored

conveniently nearby, but not on the bench or in the work space. Shellac and other combustibles—if used at all—should be stored in airtight containers away from the wood storage area.

4. Use a C-clamp or vise to hold materials firmly in place so that hands will not need to be near the business end of tools.

5. Children must keep hands safely away from where the saw might slip and cut a hand that is holding the wood.

6. Tools are used only in the woodworking area. Children should be helped to realize that tools are not toys, and can be dangerous if not properly used.

7. Hammers are for pounding nails, not people or toys. Children may not pound with the claw of the hammer because it will break.

8. Saws are only for sawing. Pounding with the saw may break its teeth. Weight on the side of a saw may bend it. A bent or rusted saw will not slide through the saw cut well. This is why saws are hung up in their places immediately after use.

9. Do not saw, hammer, or drill into the workbench or sawing bench.

10. No sharp nail points should be left protruding from the finished product. No nails are to be hammered into the bench.

11. Clear, clean, wraparound safety goggles with air vents may be worn to prevent eye injury from wood chips, sawdust, and splinters, but they often limit the child's sight and thus may themselves cause an accident.

12. Never hold nails, tacks, or screws in your mouth.

13. Never store wood with nailpoints sticking through. Pull the nails out.

14. Tools should be put down immediately if children have a disagreement.

15. Always check tools for damage and alert the children to watch for any needed repairs.

16. Children must return tools to their proper storage place, replace leftover nails in proper storage containers, and return extra lumber to the storage box or rack.

17. Children who cannot observe the limits will be asked to leave the area and find a different activity.

CHAPTER 5

Woodworking Tips and Activities

Common problems and solutions

Parents, teachers, and children sometimes encounter difficulties as they begin to work with wood. Causes and solutions for the most common problems are discussed here.

Nails bend when hammering because the workbench is too high, causing the child to hit the nail at an angle instead of directly on top. Using a solid nailing block on the floor corrects this problem. Nails that are too long or too thin will also bend (Moffitt 1973). Knots in the wood can cause weak nails to bend.

Bent nails can be straightened by holding a block of wood against the nail and hammering the nail from the side, as illustrated in Figure 23. Or the bent nail can be removed and hammered straight on a hard flat surface. If nails are bent too often, they should be discarded to avoid frustrating the child.

When wood splits while hammering, check to see if the nail is too near the edge, if the nail is too thick for the wood, or if there are too many nails in the same grain line.

To saw in a straight line, draw a line on the wood with a pencil and try square before beginning to saw (Figure 24). Also, keep the saw at a 45° angle to the wood, driving downward. Keep your eye on the cutting line, not on the saw. Remember to saw on the side of the line away from the portion of wood you want to use. If the saw cut veers away from the line, twist the saw slightly toward the line on the downward stroke.

If the wood is vibrating while being sawed, move the cutting line of the wood as close to the vise or C-clamp as possible. Using a sawing bench supports the wood better on the downward cutting thrust, preventing vibration and splitting (see Figure 5 and photo on p. 21).

Figure 23. Straightening a nail

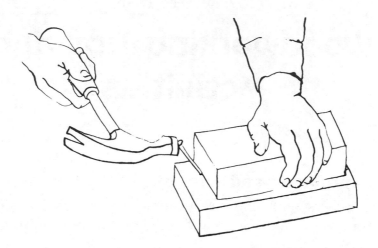

From Gilden et al. 1977, p. 15. Reprinted by permission from the National 4-H Council.

Sawing uphill can be caused by a child sawing at a workbench too high for the child's height, or by a child standing too far from the bench. Use of a low sawing bench corrects this problem.

When near the end of your saw cut, ease up on pressure and saw lightly to **prevent the wood from splitting.** Also, have someone hold the end of the board so that it does not drop and split the wood or damage the saw blade. Children can successfully cooperate with each other in this way.

Movement of the woodworking bench can be prevented by placing one side of the bench against a wall and making sure that the bench is on a level surface, or by putting rubber furniture coasters under each leg.

Related activities with wood

Children can think of countless ways in which woodworking can be used creatively and to solve classroom problems. Very young children, ages two and three years can

Figure 24. Using the try square

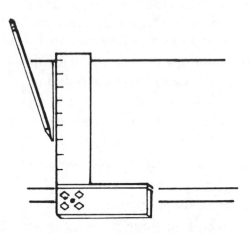

When you want to cut a line squarely across a board, use the try square. Hold the thick handle firmly along the edge of the board. Draw your pencil down the rule across the board.

From Cartwright 1975, p. 9. Reprinted by permission from the author.

- Sort and/or seriate nails or screws into containers.
- Make wood sculptures with bits of wood they have cut in various shapes and sizes and glued or nailed. Wood may be collected as scrap from lumber and woodcraft companies or earlier projects no longer needed, or it may be cut by children during practice sawing. These shapes can be painted with tempera or left natural. Children like to use gold or silver tempera.
- Some children could sandpaper and oil their creations with linseed oil. They could experiment to see how these processes bring out the beauty of the wood grain.
- Pound several nails into a short board. Encourage children to paint a design on the wood, using two or more colors. Wind string or yarn in and out of the nails to create still another design.
- Use a good tree stump or large block of wood for practice hammering.
- Smell and feel various kinds of wood. Note grain patterns, knots and other qualities.

Children about 3 1/2 years and older may also find these activities appropriate.

• In connection with block play and/or social studies, trips, or discussions, children may construct boats, trucks, airplanes, rockets, bridges, traffic signs, houses, water wheels, and many other functional models and toys.

• Use sandpaper to smooth blocks they cut from fir 2″ x 4″s. But do not mix these blocks with nursery unit blocks for building.

• When children initiate such an activity, they can make flags using scraps of fabric which they have painted and hammered or glued onto sticks, which they have cut to size.

Children five and older usually are able to engage in the following types of projects.

• Make a home for a classroom pet.

• Repair classroom equipment that has loose nails or rough edges.

• Build furniture for the dramatic play area, such as a doll bed or table, spaceship, car, boat, bridge, or traffic signs.

• Make wall hangings from scraps of wood.

Children of all ages can gain from the following activities.

• Dictate stories about their woodworking creations to an adult or older child.

• Listen to stories or read books about tools, carpenters, and building (see the Annotated Bibliography for suggested children's books).

• Participate in field trips such as a visit to a hardware store or a lumber yard to see the types of materials sold and the jobs of people working there.

• Tour a street, park, or forest to see different types of trees.

• Take a trip to a construction site when carpenters are at work. Teachers may want to preplan the visit with the carpenters so that adequate safety precautions and plans for the best learning experience can be made.

• Enjoy a visit to their classroom by a carpenter, cabinet maker, wood carver, or industrial arts teacher who demonstrates woodworking skills. Children can observe and ask questions.

Sawing and hammering can be rhythmic. Make up or adapt a song to pretend hammering during group singing but not when woodworking because it may be distracting. "The Wheels on the Bus," "If You're Happy," "Johnny Hammers with One Hammer," and "Good News" are examples of songs that can be adopted to tell about what children are doing in woodworking. For example:

> Good news! Carmen is sawing.
> Good news! Carmen is sawing.
> Good news! Carmen is sawing.
> And she's doing a real good job.
> (To the tune of "Good News")

This list indicates that all curriculum areas can be represented in woodworking: art, music, science, math, reading, language, social sciences, and physical development. Learning opportunities in all young children's programs can be extended through the challenging and valuable addition of woodworking to the curriculum.

Annotated Bibliography

Children's Books

Barton, B. *Building a House*. New York: Greenwillow, 1981.

Simply explains all the key phases in constructing a home from surveying to a family moving in. The illustrations can be the source for continued learning as children's knowledge becomes more sophisticated.

Homan, D. *In Christina's Toolbox*. Lollipop Power, P.O. Box 1171, Chapel Hill, NC 27514. 1981.

A book about a young girl's work with various tools, illustrated with drawings that show how the tools are used.

Lasson, R. *If I Had a Hammer*. New York: Dutton, 1974.

Shows middle school children and adult beginners how to correctly use seven basic tools—hammer, saw, try square, tape measure, C-clamp, Sure Form plane, and drill. Illustrated with excellent black and white photographs.

Rockwell, A., and Rockwell, H. *The Toolbox*. New York: Macmillan, 1971.

Presents the basic tools and their uses in a simple style suitable for the very young child. The illustrations are large and colorful.

Thompson, D. *Easy Wood Stuff for Kids*. Mt. Ranier, Md.: Gryphon House, 1981.

A well illustrated book of projects for children who have fairly advanced skills in woodworking.

See Catalogs.

Resources for Adults

Adams, R. J. *Creative Woodworking in the Kindergarten*. Minneapolis: T. S. Dennison, 1967.

Contains story for children useful in introducing woodworking as well as a few suggestions for simple projects.

Blackburn, G. *The Illustrated Encyclopedia of Woodworking Handtools*. New York: Simon & Schuster, 1974.

A practical reference book and guide for identifying tools. Describes the use, history, and development of handtools from the 18th century to the present.

Bramwell, M., ed. *The International Book of Wood*. New York: Simon & Schuster, 1976.
An extensive guide to wood: growth, world supply, varieties, use and treatment of 144 hardwoods and softwoods, historical significance, wildlife's use of wood, problems and techniques of woodworking, and the development of new wood products.

Cohen, D. H., and Rudolph, M. *Kindergarten and Early Schooling*. Englewood Cliffs, N.J.: Prentice-Hall, 1977.
One chapter is brief and clear on childhood needs and woodworking, with the entire book a welcome background.

Freirer, J., and Hutchings, G. *Carpentry and Building Construction*. Peoria, Ill.: Chas. A. Bennet Co., 1981.
Thorough discussion of wood, its use, availability, limits, and all major carpentry tools.

Frankle, W., ed. *Working with Wood*. Alexandria, Va.: Time-Life Books, 1979.

Jackson, A., and Day, D. *Tools and How to Use Them, an Illustrated Encyclopedia*. New York: Knopf, 1978.
Hand and power tools from ordinary to odd, their history, how they are used, how to operate them and maintain them.

Schnacke, D. *American Folk Toys: How to Make Them*. New York: Penguin Books, 1974.
Shows fascinating and imaginative toys, many easy to make, and is amply illustrated. We do not necessarily recommend them as educational, but many are fun to make and operate, especially at home.

Sloan, E. *A Museum of Early American Tools*. American Museum of Natural History. New York: Ballantine Books, 1981.
A delightfully illustrated, anecdotal yet accurate compendium of early American tools. Fascinating for adults and children alike, this book relates woodworking to American history and fosters a love for tools.

Starr, R. *Woodworking with Kids*. The Taunton Press, 52 Church Hill Rd., Box 355, Newtown, CT 06470. 1982.
A guide on woodworking technique for children five years and older. The author, an elementary school teacher, emphasizes the steps on a woodworking project, from the conception and drawing to the finished piece. Includes illustrations, many clear photographs, and a section on tools.

Swedlow, R., Lindberg, L., and Moffitt, M. *Woodworking*. Filmstrip. Early Childhood Curriculum Series No. 802. Campus Film Distributing Corp., 24 Depot Square, Tuckahoe, NY 10707. 1976.

Tangerman, E. J. *Whittling and Woodcarving.* New York: Dover Publications, 1936. $4.50 Paper (1983).
Well written, 464 illustrations, with appendix and index. It is inspiring, informative, and creative.

Catalogs

Leichtung, Inc. *The Workbench People.* 4944 Commerce Parkway, Cleveland, OH 44128. 800-321-6840.
A tool catalog with interesting hand and machine tools.

Sears Roebuck & Co. *Tool Catalog.* Catalog Department of your local store.
This catalog has pictures of many hand tools with their names. Adults can learn much from it and it is fun for children to explore, recognizing many kinds of saws, hammers, planes, files, and clamps that they could hardly include in their own shop or classroom. The teacher could remove distracting sections of the catalog which display large power tools, garden tools, etc., if desired.

Woodcraft Supply Corp. *Woodcraft Tool Catalog and Project Supply Supplement.* 313 Montvale Ave., Woburn, MA 01888. 800-225-1153.
Quality tools, pictures, and many good books listed for the expert woodworker.

Bibliography

Adkins, J. *Toolchest*. New York: Walker & Co., 1973.

Biber, B.; Shapiro E.; Wickens, D.; and Gilkeson, E. *Promoting Cognitive Growth: A Developmental-Interaction Point of View*. Washington, D.C.: National Association for the Education of Young Children, 1977.

Blackburn, G. *Illustrated Basic Carpentry*. Boston: Little, Brown, 1977.

Brandhofer, M. "Carpentry for Young Children." *Young Children* 27, no. 1 (October 1971): 17–23.

Brannen, N. *Woodworking—Competency Based Training Module #30*. Coolidge, Ariz.: Arizona HSST/CDA, n.d.

Brooke, F. *Preschool Child Development*. Athens, Ga.: Center for Continuing Education, University of Georgia, 1963.

Cartwright, S. "Trips and Blocks: A Study of Five-Year-Old Learning." Master's thesis, Bank Street College of Education, 1971.

Cartwright, S. "Blocks and Learning." *Young Children* 29, no. 3 (March 1974): 141–146.

Cartwright, S. *Classroom Carpentry, Ages 5 to 10*. Community Nursery School Press, Tenants Harbor, ME 04860. 1975. (Nine page pamphlet available free from Community Nursery School, Tenants Harbor, ME 04860.)

Cartwright, S. *What's in a Map?* New York: Coward, McCann & Geoghegan, 1976.

Cartwright, S. "Individual Pacing." Unpublished research, Community Nursery School, Tenants Harbor, ME 04860. 1982.

Clark, S., and Lyman, D., eds. *The Complete Illustrated Tool Book*. New York: Galahad, 1974.

Dewey, J. *Experience and Education*. New York: Collier-MacMillan, 1938. "Early Childhood." *Teacher*. (March 1975): 100–101.

Fuller, G. *Woodworking with Young Children*. New York: Bank Street College of Education, 1974.

Furth, H. G. *Piaget and Knowledge*. Chicago: University of Chicago Press, 1981.

Gilden, R. O.; Swiney, K. L.; Nicholls, J. M.; Barquest, G.; Palmer, E.; Crawford, P.; and Olson, E. A. *Adventures in Woodworking, Unit 1 Members' Manual*. Chicago: National 4-H Council, 1977.

Gilden, R. O.; Swiney, K. L.; Nicholls, J. M.; Barquest, G.; Palmer, E.; Crawford, P.; and Olson, E. A. *Learning and Building, Unit 2 Members' Manual*. Chicago: National 4-H Council, 1975.

Gilden, R. O.; Swiney, K. L.; Nicholls, J. M.; Barquest, G.; Palmer, E.; Crawford, P.; and Olson, E. A. *Building Bigger Things, Unit 3 Members' Manual.* Chicago: National 4-H Council, 1973.

Greenberg, P. *Do-It-Yourself Staff Growth Program.* Washington, D.C.: The Growth Program. 1975.

Hendrick, J. *Total Learning for the Whole Child.* St. Louis: Mosby, 1980.

Hirsch, E. S. *The Block Book.* Washington, D.C.: National Association for the Education of Young Children, 1984.

Lasky, L., and Mukerji, R. *Art: Basic for Young Children.* Washington, D.C.: National Association for the Education of Young Children, 1980.

Lawrence, M. *Working with Wood.* New York: Crowell, 1979.

Moffitt, M. W. *Woodworking for Children.* New York: Early Childhood Education Council, 1973.

Osborn, K., and Haupt, D. *Creative Activities for Young Children.* Detroit, Mich.: The Merrill-Palmer Institute, 1964.

Piaget, J., and Inhelder, B. *The Early Growth of Logic in the Child.* New York: Norton, 1964.

Pitcher, E. G.; Lasher, M. G.; Feinburg, S. G.; and Braun, L. A. *Helping Young Children Learn,* 3rd ed. Columbus, Ohio; Merrill, 1979.

Shea, J. G. *Woodworking for Everybody,* 4th ed. New York: Van Nostrand Reinhold, 1970.

Snyder, A., and Biber, B. *How Do We Know a Good Teacher?* Publication No. 61. New York: Bank Street College of Education, 1965.

Stone, J. G. *A Guide to Discipline.* Washington, D.C.: National Association for the Education of Young Children, 1978.

Torre, F. D. *Woodworking for Kids.* Garden City, N.Y.: Doubleday, 1978.

Conducting a Woodworking Workshop for Teachers and Parents

by Anita Payne Garner and Patsy Skeen

Getting ready

The model presented here, based on the first part of this book, contains suggestions for conducting a four to five hour woodworking workshop for teachers of young children, parents, and students. Such a workshop should be led by someone who feels comfortable in assuming a leadership role and has skills in communication and woodworking. Workshop leaders are encouraged to modify this guide to meet their needs and the needs of the group.

Objectives

1. To enhance personal skills in woodworking.
2. To help participants recognize the value of woodworking as a learning activity for young children.
3. To examine factors related to planning woodworking activities such as
    a. materials and equipment selection, use, storage, and care
    b. teacher role
    c. setting up a woodworking area
    d. children's developmental abilities
    e. safety precautions
4. To present curriculum ideas for woodworking.

Assessment and planning

To prepare for the workshop
1. Read the first part of this book.

2. Assess the needs of your group by using a questionnaire or discussion with participants. Consider each participant's past experience, skills to be developed, feelings about woodworking, and personal goals.

3. The Teacher Evaluation Checklist (see p. 82) can be used to preassess as well as evaluate teacher competencies after the workshop.

4. Develop your objectives, agenda, and workshop plan based on this assessment information.

5. Gather the necessary materials, equipment, handouts, and other aids well in advance.

6. Notify participants of the time and location of the workshop at least three weeks in advance. Confirm the arrangements again two days before the workshop is to be held.

7. Make child care arrangements for staff and parents.

8. Set up the work area and audio-visual aids before the workshop participants arrive.

Group size

A small group of 20 or less gives each participant an opportunity to express ideas, ask questions, and have ample hands-on use of the materials. Adults learn by doing just like children. For larger groups, assistant workshop leaders can be selected.

Materials and equipment

- name tags
- sign-in sheet
- evaluation sheets
- handouts
- chalkboard and chalk or flip chart and markers
- adult seating
- screen
- cassette tape recorder
- slide or filmstrip projector
- self-made woodworking slides or a filmstrip presentation such as *Woodworking* (Swedlow, Lindberg, and Moffitt 1976)
- one bench and one set of tools for each group of three to four adults including
  - 7 to 10 ounce claw hammer
  - 305mm to 405mm (12" to 16") crosscut saw
  - assorted nails with wide heads, 25mm to 75mm (1" to 3") in length, including wire, box, and roofing nails.

- medium grade (100 grit) sandpaper mounted on a wooden block
- C-clamp, if workbench is not equipped with a vise
- optional tools such as pliers, try square, screwdriver 100mm to 150mm (4″ to 6″) long with 6mm (1/4″) blade, block plane, metric measure, hand drill, bit and brace
- assortment of suitable woods (see p. 10)
- assortment of wood unsuitable for children and wood products (see p. 10)
- accessory materials such as those listed on pp. 42 – 44
- display of children's woodwork (optional)
- refreshments

Preworkshop activities

Ask participants to read the first part of this book.

Workshop plan

Activity/method	Materials needed
Registration. Participants sign in, receive name tags and agendas. (10 minutes)	sign-in sheet, pen, name tags, marker, agendas, small table
Welcome and introductions. To set a friendly tone, use a technique such as asking participants to choose a partner and to chat informally for 5 minutes. Partners then introduce each other to the whole group. (15 minutes)	
Workshop objectives. Review objectives on flip chart or chalkboard. Invite participants to modify them. Display objectives throughout the session. (5 minutes)	objectives printed on flip chart or chalkboard
Display woodworking tools/equipment. Invite participants to examine the materials and suggest that they think of ways to use them. Ask them to express their feelings about letting young children use adult tools (Greenberg 1975). Make yourself available for questions. (10–15 minutes)	workbenches, tools, accessory materials, wood

continued on next page

Workshop plan, continued

Activity/method	Materials needed
Do-it session. Divide into work groups of two or three. The leader should move from group to group, demonstrating techniques, to help participants start experimenting with the tools (Greenberg 1975). (30–45 minutes)	work area for each group
Sharing session. Participants can display and discuss their work. Ask each group to talk about difficulties they experienced in using the tools and materials and their solutions to problems (Greenberg 1975). Demonstrate solutions for problems (see pp. 65–66). (30–60 minutes)	
Discussion on values of woodworking. Divide participants into groups of four. Ask them to develop a list of the concepts and skills they think children would have an opportunity to develop through working with wood (Moffitt 1973). Suggest that each group select a recorder to write down their ideas and present them to the entire group. (15 minutes)	chart paper, markers
Small group reports on values of woodworking. Ask one group to share their listing of skills/concepts with the whole group. Other groups can add to the list. The leader can compile the master list. Then ask the group to discuss why woodworking is used infrequently or sometimes not at all in programs for young children (Greenberg 1975). (15 minutes)	flip chart, markers
Audio-visual presentation—planning and implementing woodworking. Use one of the suggested audio-visual aids to present information about planning and implementing woodworking activities. Encourage participants to comment, to offer additional suggestions, and to ask questions. (20–25 minutes)	screen, projector, cassette recorder, extension cords, filmstrip or your own slides

continued on next page

Workshop plan, continued

Activity/method	Materials needed
Role playing situations. Divide participants into groups of about seven. Assign each group one of the role playing situations outlined in Appendix A. Ask each small group to present one of the role playing situations to the whole group. (15–45 minutes)	role playing sheets (see Appendix A)
Wrap-up. Review workshop objectives with participants to determine if they have been accomplished. Distribute and discuss evaluation forms. Collect completed evaluation forms. (5–10 minutes)	objectives printed on flip chart, evaluation forms (see Appendix B)

Alternatives

If participants have had little experience in woodworking, more time to practice with tools and wood is needed. A second two hour practice period could be added to the workshop—perhaps after the small group reports concerning the values of woodworking or at the end of the workshop. Periodic practical follow-up workshops are also useful.

Instructors of early childhood curriculum courses could arrange for students to observe children involved in woodworking activities *before* introducing audio-visual or lecture material in class. If class scheduling does not allow enough time for an actual experience in working with wood during class time, set up woodworking tools and equipment in another room. Assign students time to use these materials as part of the laboratory requirement of the course. As a final assignment, students could be expected to plan, carry out, and evaluate a woodworking activity with young children.

A shorter version of the workshop can also be developed for parents who are interested in learning about the value of woodworking experiences for children. Parents also need to be reassured that woodworking can be a safe activity for children. Whether parents are interested in doing woodworking with children or simply understanding the value of woodworking, it is recommended that they have an opportunity to work with wood. Teachers can set up a display of the children's woodworking products (Brannen, n.d.)

Evaluation

Even the most experienced teacher can benefit from periodic on-site visits by a curriculum consultant, workshop leader, or other supervisory personnel who can observe woodworking activities, answer questions, and offer suggestions and encouragement. Supervisors in competency-based teacher education programs may wish to use the following Teacher Evaluation Checklist to assess skills. Teachers can also use the checklist to evaluate themselves.

Teacher evaluation checklist

	Yes	No	Needs improvement
Values			
1. Can the teacher list at least five of the values of woodworking for the young child?			
Equipment and materials (Brannen, n.d.)			
1. Can the teacher demonstrate knowledge of the equipment and materials needed in a woodworking center for young children?			
a. essential equipment, type and size of tools			
b. importance of proper height of workbench			
c. use of a sawing bench and nailing base			
d. kind of nails			
e. kind of wood best suited for use by young children			
f. accessories desirable			
2. Has the teacher developed a plan for the proper care and storage of equipment and materials?			
Teacher role and guidance			
1. Does the teacher demonstrate an understanding of differences in children's developmental needs, abilities, and interests?			
2. Is the teacher able to determine when adult help is needed?			

	Yes	No	Needs improvement
3. Is the teacher responsive to signs of children's fatigue and frustration?			
4. Does the teacher use methods and materials which enable the children to experience success?			
5. Are children allowed (within reasonable limits) to experiment and use their own ideas in working with wood?			
6. Does the teacher model proper care and use of tools and equipment?			
7. Can the teacher demonstrate how to solve particular woodworking problems? (see p. 65)			
8. Does the teacher frequently offer woodworking activities to children?			
9. Does the teacher integrate art, music, science, language, reading, number concepts, social science, and physical development into woodworking activities?			
Safety			
1. Is direct supervision of one adult for two children provided?			
2. Is the workbench kept clear of tools and materials not in use?			
3. Is the workbench sturdy and equipped with a vise or C-clamp?			
4. Are tools and equipment checked before use?			
5. Are tools stored where they cannot be reached when a teacher is not available to supervise?			
6. Are children not involved in woodworking far enough away from the work area?			
7. Are limits for woodworking clear to adults and children?			
8. Are rules for woodworking firmly and consistently enforced?			

Suggested Role Playing Situations

Situation 1

Mrs. Chandler has asked for a conference with you. As the conference begins, it is quite noticeable that she is angry and upset about the woodworking activities offered by your program. She thinks it is unsafe and makes her feelings known. She doesn't think the children are learning anything either. How would you handle this situation? It may be helpful to begin your discussion by reviewing the skills children learn and the safety considerations related to woodworking. Discuss what could be done, and then choose two people to role play your solution.

Situation 2

Tom and Melinda are working at the woodworking bench. Several of the other children start to crowd around the workbench. You remind the children of the rule about only two children at the workbench at one time, but the children are so interested in the activity that they don't seem to be hearing you. Meanwhile, Melinda is getting angry because the crowding is interfering with her work. All of a sudden she raises the hammer in a threatening manner toward the other children. How should the situation be handled? Discuss ways this situation could be avoided. Develop a listing of specific limits for children working with wood. Role play the situation with the solution.

Situation 3

You are a group of teachers who are meeting to plan the equipment needed and the set-up for the woodworking area for next year. There are several options discussed concerning the best arrangement and storage of equipment and tools, for example, inside, outside, in the room, in a special room. Discuss the pros and cons of each suggestion and come up with the best plan for your center. During your discussion, develop a listing of the equipment and tools you will need. Role play the situation illustrating how you arrived at the best plan.

Sample Workshop Evaluation Form

1. What have you found most helpful about this session?

2. Least helpful?

3. What have you gained from this session that will help you as a teacher?

4. What changes in this presentation would have helped you to gain more from this session?

5. What suggestions do you have for future workshops?

References

Brannen, N. *Woodworking—Competency Based Training Module #30.* Coolidge, Ariz.: Arizona HSST/CDA, n.d.

Greenberg, P. *Do-It-Yourself Staff Growth Program.* Washington, D.C.: The Growth Program, 1975.

Moffitt, M. W. *Woodworking for Children.* New York: Early Childhood Education Council, 1973.

Swedlow, R.; Lindberg, L.; and Moffitt, M. *Woodworking.* Filmstrip. Early Childhood Curriculum Series No. 802. Campus Film Distributing Corp., 24 Depot Square, Tuckahoe, NY 10707. 1976.

Information about NAEYC

NAEYC is . . .
. . . a membership-supported organization of people committed to fostering the growth and development of children from birth through age eight. Membership is open to all who share a desire to serve and act on behalf of the needs and rights of young children.

NAEYC provides . . .
. . . educational services and resources to adults who work with and for children, including

Young Children, the Journal for early childhood educators

Books, posters, brochures and videos to expand your knowledge and commitment to young children, with topics including infants, curriculum, research, discipline, teacher education, and parent involvement

An **Annual Conference** that brings people from all over the country to share their expertise and advocate on behalf of children and families

Week of the Young Child celebrations sponsored by NAEYC Affiliate Groups across the country to call public attention to the needs and rights of children and families.

Insurance plans for individuals and programs

Public affairs information for knowledgeable advocacy efforts at all levels of government and through the media

The **National Academy of Early Childhood Programs,** a voluntary accreditation system for high-quality programs for children

The **Child Care Information Service,** a centralized source of information-sharing, distribution, and collaboration

For free information about membership, publications, or other NAEYC services . . .
. . . call NAEYC at 202-232-8777 or 800-424-2460 or write to NAEYC, 1834 Connecticut Avenue, N.W., Washington, DC 20009-5786.